KATE BROWNLEY is a voice  everybody's life coach and works as runs her own social media account Instagram, posting a quote a day to morning off right.

Her experiences have shaped her into becoming the woman she is today; heart-warming stories are shared from deep within and portrayed in a manner that anyone can relate to. This book includes her inspirational quotes, creative stories and exercises that she has designed to help your mind blossom.

Kate has turned her whole life around by following what she sets out in this book. She has reached a turning point and wants the same for you. For more motivation, follow Kate on Instagram @rewiringthoughts_ and begin your journey today!

To Tony

Thank you for being that for me!

Lots of love

Kate

IT HAS ALWAYS BEEN WITHIN YOU

KATE BROWNLEY

SilverWood

Published in 2021 by SilverWood Books

SilverWood Books Ltd
14 Small Street, Bristol, BS1 1DE, United Kingdom
www.silverwoodbooks.co.uk

ISBN 978-1-80042-125-7 (paperback)
ISBN 978-1-80042-126-4 (ebook)

British Library Cataloguing in Publication Data
A CIP catalogue record for this book is
available from the British Library

Page design and typesetting by SilverWood Books

Find yourself

~~~~~~~~~~~~~

Find yourself within this book.

Find yourself within the pages.

Find the answers within yourself.

'And all she needed to do was to believe in herself.'

Introduction

I was the girl who read all books; it was my favourite thing to do. Reading brought sunshine to my rainy days and made my heart feel warm inside. Every page had a different story to tell – just like you and me. We each have a story of our own, whether that be to help uplift one another or a story that can save somebody's life or even bring us realisation of our own self-worth. My own personal stories are what have brought me to write at this very moment. I hope this book can grant reflection on your journey and inspire you for what lies ahead.

This book will show you that you can become whoever you want to be; that anything is possible if you work for it. If I could go back to my thirteen-year-old self and tell her how life would turn out, I am not quite sure she would believe me. The girl who read the books certainly became the woman who wrote them – a woman with a hope to inspire the lives of others from something deep within her soul, a soul passionately ready to help others seek and reach their full potential.

It all began when I started one of my first jobs in which I had to interact with the public on a daily basis. What was so alarming was that so many people I had engaged with spoke of their personal issues, whether it be insecurities, an illness or a broken relationship. Speaking with these people, I found myself giving advice from my own perspective and leaving them feeling better than when they walked in. Their faces would light up, and some would return on another day to let me know how much their mood had improved since our little chat. It was a visible change, a shift in their energy and body language. Watching their self-confidence blossom, as a spectator on the sidelines, truly touched me.

At first I had no idea it was I who had had this impact on someone else's life. I thought it was morally right to be friendly, plus I was just doing my job. As it became a common occurrence, it was clear there was a hidden ability within me to help others see their true potential. It felt as though an ember was alight deep in my stomach, and every time I helped others the flame grew bigger and bigger. Something else I learned about this flame was that it could be sparked into others and spread like wildfire. Not only did the flame grow in me but in everyone else I came into contact with, showing others' their true potential and also mine – a new-found passion that will last forever. It gives me goosebumps as I sit here at my laptop and write these very words – I feel free. Time stops when I write, and my mind wanders into another world. Now fate has brought you and me together. My words are here to inspire you and give you a new perception.

You know that small flame I mentioned? I want to ignite it in your stomach. It will be up to you how much it grows. This is your opportunity to accept this journey and the substantial growth it holds. Every answer you need is there; it has always been within you. I promise that this book will help you find yourself. It will teach you that it's okay not to be okay at times and to hold on and appreciate those special moments. I have overcome so many hurdles on my own personal journey and I am the happiest I've been for years. I want the same for you. By reading this, you have the chance to get to that level by letting go of bad habits and bringing in the new, which will make you realise your worth on this planet. Now that we are acquainted, it gives me the greatest pleasure to say: my friend, let's make the world a better place together.

Before we start, I ask you to grab a pen and highlight any sentences or quotes that make you feel inspired. Let this book become your new smartphone. Let it give you that boost of confidence you have been searching for. Are you ready to come on the road of self-discovery? I think you are, so let's go…

When I was a little girl, I always wanted to be someone great. I just didn't know what that greatness was. When I think back to my years as a child, I was no different to other children. I was silly and innocent and always wanting to play. I danced from the age of five, which helped me express myself in so many ways – it was my life. I didn't focus much at school, never giving it the attention I should have. I was too fixated on my dancing and not my grades. I mean, that's not a bad thing, because I was focused on something! After not getting high marks at school, I left and went straight into dance college. Shock. It was going great for twelve months, but suddenly that road was coming to an end. One day I had to say goodbye to dancing, because my back couldn't take it any longer. I will never forget the doctor turning around and saying, 'You need to find a new hobby, like jigsaw puzzling.' The blood rushed through my body as I screamed out, roaring in my head, 'NO, NO, NO.' My whole world came crashing down. The one dream I had, the only thing I felt exceptional at in my life, I was told to move away from it. In the years that followed, I searched as an adult to find my dream, my purpose; but how could I find something I already thought I had? I was lost, not knowing in which direction to go. I knew I had always loved being around people, and here is where it led me in my professional career: to retail. As time went by, I couldn't see clearly enough what my purpose was, but deep down I felt a heavy heart because I knew my desire was burning for more.

Anything is possible

You are capable of doing so many amazing things.

Even if you can't see it,

You can do it.

You were born to be great.

This is your reminder: you can do it, beautiful.

Acceptance

'Acceptance means you accept the good and the bad. You take somebody for who they are by letting things just be as they are and welcoming the things you cannot change.'

@rewiringthoughts_

I have always worn my heart on my sleeve – a cliché, I know. Putting everyone before myself and craving the approval of others. My life would be in the palms of somebody else's hands and my soul felt trapped between their fingers, as if they were steel bars in a prison and I was waiting for the day I would be released. Lost in the bubble of other people's comfort, every day was like waiting in the wrong place for a bus that would never arrive. I allowed their words to direct me into a world of misunderstanding my own self-worth.

Growing up, people walked all over me, or as my nan would say, "shit on me" plenty of times. I was the girl who was always "too nice" or "too kind". When I was younger, sticking up for myself was tough. I was intimidated by everyone and was scared of answering back. I was my own shadow, holding back when I had so much to give. My nan was right – I did get shat on. She always told me to stand up for myself – don't let anybody mess you around! This, however, is easier said than done, especially when you are a teenager eager to fit in. I coped with school life and rarely mixed with other girls, thinking I wasn't cool or popular enough because nobody made me feel of any importance. Every day attending school was a chore I detested. Walking to the bus stop, crying inside, wishing I could fast-forward my life five years, just because school would hopefully become a distant memory…right?

I do admit, though, the struggle to express myself kept me from trying to do better at socialising and left me on mute throughout my school years. People didn't know who I was because they didn't make time to get to know Katie. I would feel so uncomfortable around others, coming home deflated to my nan because there had been no progress from the day before. It drove me to questioning: 'Why aren't I good enough?' I believed that if no one found interest in me, then of course something must be wrong with me. Must I really become the person who I know will get attention, even if it's not the wonderful Katie I have bottled inside? The simple answer is "no"; but, for a teenage girl, nothing is simple.

It took so many years to emerge from the deep ocean that was anxiety, not understanding how I got so caught up in it, and drowning for so long. Now I look back and realise that the only person I wasn't accepting was myself, too afraid to show others who I really was. So what if there was a day when I didn't hear about the two best friends Rosie and Lisa falling out for the 900th time? Did I really need to be involved and should I have taken it so personally? Of course not. Accept the little things and carry on with your life. This is what would have made my character blossom, not letting minor school occurrences get the better of me. If I had followed this simple motto in my school days, socially it would have been a walk in the park! Back then I was my own victim, too young to understand my importance and the impact I could bring to this world. As the beautiful and confident woman I am today, I look in the mirror and smile because I know what I'm worth and I am as sure as hell about what I can give to others.

You are not labelled as something forever. You can be whatever you believe your worth is in this world. Don't be scared to walk this life alone by being who you really are. People's opinions of you are reflections of themselves, and guess what? They change constantly! You have to concentrate on your own path and never let anyone dull your sparkle, because you were born to contribute your unique qualities to this world. It's time to focus on you.

This journey

This journey you are about to start will make you feel lost; or maybe you feel it now.

Every time we lose ourselves we are reborn, bigger and better.

This isn't going to be easy, but I promise it will be worth it.

A fresh start will bring forward a new you, viewing the world through a new lens, seeing things you never thought were possible.

This journey will take you above and beyond, healing what's inside, and when you look back at your old life you will never want to revisit it.

This new beginning is just the start of you.

Accepting who we are

I came across a quote a few years ago that said, 'There will never be another you, and that is your superpower.' I mean, wow! This quote inspired me above and beyond. Think about that: no matter how long the world goes on for, there will never be another creation that is exactly the same organism as you. It's crazy to even comprehend, isn't it? We are only here once, and nobody else will even come close to being like us. It's this very concept that can make a person struggle to embrace who they really are.

Why is it we find it so hard to look in the mirror and say, 'Holy shit, I look fantastic today'? When somebody pays us a compliment, why do we not believe them? Has it really come to the point where "thank you" is an automatic response, without really considering where the admiration stemmed from? Is there a genuine dislike for ourselves, meaning that we don't digest flattering and warm comments? Just like that we turn a blind eye, assuming it to be politeness. 'They don't really think my outfit is cute. They are just saying it because they tell everyone that', or 'They talk a load of nonsense'. You see, we take the compliment we receive and question the person who gives it.

We spend so much time comparing ourselves to others that we become numb to our own existence. If we don't pay any attention to who we really are then that leaves me with the following questions for you: are you living or are you just floating through life? Are you paying any attention to who you see in the mirror? Do you really know who that person is? There was a time once when I did not. Even to look at myself in the mirror and smile brought me so much disgust. Not being able to draw my attention away from the flaws in my appearance. My spots staring back at me telling me how ugly I was.

Every time I washed my face I could feel the lumps on my chin, and that would dig me deeper into a hole of insecurity I dug for myself. Every time I went to the doctor's, I would leave with a new cream or antibiotic, praying my skin would clear. I would pay stupid amounts of money for private skincare, putting every ounce of belief I had in me into every product I bought and hoping this was my ticket to clear skin, back to the standard we expect of ourselves. The problem was I never reached that destination and it always came down to hormones. It was such a vicious circle. Off I was, back on that horse which took me round and round in circles until I was left dazed by self-loathing and insecurity. The only way it would stop was if I jumped off the horse. So that's exactly what I did: I jumped off. I was sick to death of putting myself down, so I practised my self-talk, and from that moment everything changed. At first, talking in the mirror felt strange – even smiling made me cringe – but as time went on it got to a point were talking to myself grew a confidence within, I became a new person, one for the better.

Every time that little voice inside my head crept up, telling me I wasn't good or pretty enough, I shut it down as soon as it came, and I would go to the mirror and practice my affirmations. I had to break free from the mindset of thinking I wasn't good enough – and so do you. Get comfortable with the uncomfortable, and that's where you will grow. Don't give that little voice inside your head control of your attention – it tells you made-up information just to bring you down.

You are stronger than these negative thoughts, so don't take them too personally; and remember you have the power to free yourself from these comments. Start your journey of self-love, even if it isn't a pretty sight at first. It gets messy very quickly, but the most beautiful thing about it is that you come back to life more fulfilled after you have taken the time to put your well-being first. The grass becomes greener where you water it, and the seeds grow where you plant them. Then the good gets better, and guess what? You begin living.

'The only setting you need to change is your attitude.'

@rewiringthoughts_

10 daily affirmations to help with acceptance

1. I accept I will have my down days, and when I do I will talk to myself with more love and kindness

2. I accept and love my body for what it is; I will always treat it with care

3. I accept myself for all my flaws and imperfections; I am beautiful just the way I am

4. I accept I am worthy of all blessings and abundance

5. I accept I am deserving of all new opportunities

6. I accept I will make mistakes; I am ready to learn from them

7. I accept I am in control of making myself happy

8. I accept others for being who they are

9. I accept the things I can't control

10. I accept that what I focus on I bring into my life

It all starts with you

It was said by Dr Maxwell Maltz that it takes 21 days to form a new habit. So, below, I challenge you to write down ten affirmations about the areas of your life where you feel insecure. Pick one out from your ten that is most relevant to you. Say it out loud every morning in the mirror until the statement sounds right. You will usually start to feel some sort of emotion after your fifth time. To begin with, aim to say it ten times in the mirror. Continue this for seven days and, I guarantee, by the end of the week you will be stating the affirmation only a few times before you believe it. For the following week, choose another one of your affirmations that seems applicable and follow the process again. It will become more natural second time round and by the third week you will be a pro. This is important because after completing the challenge you will only use the affirmations when appropriate. They will be more effective than any other method used previously to deal with problems which have weighed you down throughout life – it will become second nature.

Once you speak more kindly to yourself you will notice the impact it has on your mood. Seems easy, I know, but it takes daily encouragement to put these habits in place. At first it will feel uncomfortable, because your mind has been used to you neglecting it for so long; but literally from out of nowhere there will be a virtual click, and from then on the belief will grow.

You can trick your brain into believing anything, but it is the type of energy you fuel it with that matters. Once you can maintain positive talk, there is a level of new-found self-appreciation for who you are. What makes this so special? Well, most importantly, it will strengthen the relationship with yourself, setting a pathway for having more control over what goes on in your life. Be ecstatic! You will have acquired a skill whereby speaking to yourself in small pep talks for motivation vibrates out to those around you, as if you are a leader. Shout out those affirmations which have been hidden deep inside but have always lingered. Say it, believe it, say it, believe it! You probably had one or two ideas that came to mind when I introduced this exercise (let me guess – it stemmed from a new year's resolution) but now, when addressing these problems, they're starting to appear to the surface after thought, aren't they? Write them down in clear and vocal statements. Now begins your 21-day challenge.

Your 10 daily affirmations

1. ....

2. ....

3. ....

4. ....

5. ....

6. ....

7. ....

8. ....

9. ....

10. ....

Repeat after me

She is beautiful.

She is strong.

She is enough.

Knowing

I am loved.

I am important.

I make a difference.

Accepting somebody else's life choices

Isn't it funny how we can choose to take on somebody else's drama and make it feel like it is our own? We get wrapped up in situations that have absolutely nothing to do with us. We take on too many problems and then question why so much conflict is coming to us. Let me share with you a story about a friend of mine and her boyfriend. I will openly admit I did not like him. I felt uneasy in his presence, knowing what he would get up to behind my friend's back. I couldn't get my head around the fact that she always went back to him, especially after his wandering eyes for anyone. Eurgh! I couldn't stand him. Every time I saw his face it would infuriate me, the blood rushing to the surface of my skin. I mean, come on, he cheated on her! I would watch the tears stream down my friend's face and watch her cry for hours on end – going through another heartbreaking story. It was painful.

I would stay up until 3am, in full flow on that "best friend lecture vibe", desperately wanting her to realise what she is worth. Twenty minutes later, however, I would realise it's like throwing shit at a wall and hoping some of it sticks. I would think, 'This is it, she isn't going back this time,' as we slumped to bed, both drained from the whole situation. It would all be a waste the next day after waking up in the afternoon to find out she had already planned a Nando's date with him. I wonder, what made them choose Nando's to make up? The food is delicious, to be fair.

They both were back and forth like a yoyo, always escalating so quickly from one end to the other. To see her play happy families as I watched from the sidelines only caused more pain for me. From that moment I realised this was my friend's issue to deal with, not mine. What good was I doing by not accepting this? I was only disappointing myself by voicing my opinions and feeling hurt, as if I was her inner conscience who had control over her choices. As soon as I accepted this, a huge weight lifted from my shoulders. I felt in a better state of mind.

We have to truly understand that we each have our own life to live. We may not agree with the idea of seeing our family and friends suffer with their choices, but we have to tell ourselves: 'It is not my life to judge.' Let people be people in order to find their happiness. For your friends and family, just show you support them whatever their decision. As long as you're there, they will appreciate that more than anything, whether that be the next day or in years to come. It is not our mess to clean up, so detach yourself from other people's chaos and let them discover the answers for themselves. We each have our own lives to live and we have to follow our own hearts.

We are all free

~~~~~~~~~

To live life exactly how we want it.

Let others do what makes them happy,

While you do what makes you happy.

And they all lived happily ever after.

Accepting the things we can't control

How many times have we let scenarios we can't control control us? You're leaving for work in a panic to catch your train, which departs in eight minutes. You're a ten-minute walk away. Arriving very flustered after the half-hearted jog to avoid looking silly – yet still appearing to be participating in a racewalk – you see the train operator blow his whistle as he glares into your eyes, almost as if he gets a kick out of knowing you will be late. Well, isn't that just great? Cold waiting room it is. The second the train turns up (thank God) you jump on, only to see a sea of heads, like a tin of sardines.

Every seat is taken, and you are left balancing uneasily in the middle, avoiding that accidental knock into someone else. As you attempt to evade eye contact with every single person, it becomes almost impossible not to focus on the woman eating her home-made tuna baguette very noisily. To add more fuel to the fire, you hate the smell of tuna. It's the one day you wish your nose was blocked! With your teeth gritted, and holding your breath as you count down the seconds until you get off this train journey of hell, you reach your destination. Another racewalk and you will be no more than ten minutes late. Shirt untucked, bags twisted and juggling everything else in your hands, you're out of breath as you enter the building. Who do you bump into first? Your manager. Brilliant! As you prepare yourself for a reprimand, they actually smile and greet you, but with a confused look on their face. 'You're in early – your shift doesn't start for another hour!' And there it is: the final blow! You're ready to scream. All of that for nothing, and the day feels ruined before it has begun. Little did you know that the power to change this day around was within your control all along.

Why is it that the things we can't control trigger our emotions so deeply? Why do we let unimportant matters bring us down? It is so much easier to moan about life instead of being positive and letting things be as they are. We start off our day as monsters in the world because we allow so many things to anger us. To set ourselves up for a miserable day, we give our full attention to the things we have no control over, putting newly found aggravations to the top of our well-thought-out plans for the day. Why do we respond as if this is a personal attack, creating it as a problem? When you take a step back, you will realise you don't have to let these situations enter your state of mind and snowball into over-exaggerations. It is not your responsibility to invite every little thing to bombard your inner space, but it is your obligation to decide what attitude to take with regard to the things you can't control.

You can make adjustments to where your attention is focused, and take the opportunity to flip that supposed negative around. Play and sing along to your favourite music as you sit there in a traffic jam, walk on along the pavement where the sun is shining, call that one person you know will make you smile – the list is endless. You have to make the best out of these situations, because they won't be there forever. Not every day will go as planned, and that's okay. It's how you control your response that can improve your day more than the plans you originally had. My best practice for this is to speak to myself and say, 'It's not a problem unless I make it one.' This "it is what it is" mentality changes everything. Your vocabulary has such a huge influence on the brain. Next time you catch yourself in this situation, recall these pages and the story that came with them. It will help you accept not just those crammed train journeys with the tuna baguette lady but the deeper issues that many struggle to let go of. Nobody is holding you back but yourself. You have the power to enjoy the present moment. So why don't you?

Two scenarios of acceptance

Negative: *'I can't believe the weather today. It has spoilt everything for me.'*

Positive: 'Ah well, the weather isn't the best but it is what it is. I will still make this day the greatest day ever.'

Negative: *'I hate my body. I never have time to work out.'*

Positive: 'I will prioritise and make time to get my workouts in. I love and care for my body.'

Control

I may not be able to control

Everything that happens around me, but

I shall control my response,

Attitude and gratitude for this life, the only one I have.

Accepting we can't control what other people think and say about us

I used to think I could control what others thought about me. It led me to concentrate harder on those who least deserved it. Being extra cordial would automatically set them up to like me. Except this wasn't the case. I was a people pleaser. This façade was slowly eating me up, and I knew it was time for change. The growth that I have today wouldn't be there if I hadn't set myself free from this obsession for admiration. It became such a routine that I would agree topics in conversations just to please others, without having any understanding of what they were preaching. It would go something along the lines of:

> **Friend:** *'I don't believe in—'*
> **Me:** *'Yeah yeah, me too.'*
> or
> **Friend:** *'I prefer my hair this colour, but I am thinking of getting this done. What do you think?'*
> **Me:** *'Yeah, I agree with you. The hair you have now is better.'*

Even writing this now, I can't believe I didn't notice this downward spiral, but when you are in a rut, how are you supposed to? I was copying what others would say in order to get their approval, which in turn made my uncertainty grow as to who I was. I used to put everyone above myself, favouring others because I thought it would make me grow into a better person. It took me a long time to realise this isn't how strong relationships are formed. After keeping this habit going for so long, the realisation smacked me in the face one day: you can't control what people say or think about you.

Although I knew a transformation was necessary, I was struggling to find a way to start, but the breakthrough happened at a friend's birthday. Nothing particularly happened at this party other than the usual gossip that is passed around at these events. The only problem was that it involved me. People were spreading rumours. 'She's been saying this about you, and she said that.' I remember feeling sick to the stomach hearing those remarks, because this "friend" was one of the people I would put more effort into being kind towards – wearing my heart on my sleeve and supporting all her choices. I know you shouldn't believe everything you hear, so at this party I went over and asked my so-called friend if this was true. Her response said it all. In that split second I rushed over to the bathroom, and stared at myself in the mirror and my inner voice immediate replied, without overthinking (as I quite regularly did), was: 'Who cares what she thinks? She clearly isn't a true friend to talk behind your back.' As simple as that.

Those words were like a switch that made a lightbulb flicker on in my head. It was all I needed to hear. I remember feeling instant embarrassment. Not from the quick lecture from myself but from the actions I had been taking for so long to deal with relationships and interaction. Something clicked with me that night. After taking a step back from these brainwashed thoughts, I stopped myself. I realised that, no matter how kindly I treat others, no matter what I agree on, whether I want to or not, you can't control what people say or think about you. These people didn't value me or the time I gave them, and instead threw me away like an out-of-fashion dress.

Isn't it funny how we can look back on scenarios – seeing them for what they really are when we finally come out of them? You realise a friendship, or the relationship with your ex, was toxic. I carried my own words with me and repeated them in my head. 'Who cares what she thinks?' The craving of validation from others would happen no more! Something snapped inside me – I didn't care who came up to me that night or about any other petty comments that were getting made. Choosing to rise above this by removing oneself from fake surroundings is the best thing to be done for self-growth.

If you focus on other people's perceptions more than your own, it will only create someone who isn't really you. Screaming to the world 'Like me, love me' is basically handing your humanity over on a silver plate, and this will only disconnect from that character inside you. This creates a hatred of existing, because self-doubt causes questioning as to whether you are good enough. You wouldn't turn your back on somebody else. So think of that somebody as yourself. I promise: the moment you stop giving yourself labels you wouldn't give others, self-acceptance happens, and it will grow a strong love for who you are.

Ask these questions: does this person give the support I need for our friendship and do they fit into the life I want to create? Do I feel good around these people or not? If not, walk away and free yourself. Find people on your wavelength. I say this because you deserve to have the right people around you, sharing the same love you give to them. Don't complicate it. Build up your self-esteem by talking more kindly to yourself and a new-found respect will begin to flourish. Eventually, others will follow. Self-respect comes with standing up for number one: YOU. When there is disrespect, be conscious of it. Take the moral high ground by removing yourself from that environment and you will leave with pride. From that point onwards, your philosophy for the power of self-love will only expand from the understanding that you deserve so much more.

Practices focused on emotional well-being have become massively accepted worldwide, and for a good reason. Your Mental Health should be your main priority. You live with your own mind 24/7 and, just like the other organs in the body, the brain needs to be looked after. If there is something that doesn't compute with your beliefs in comparison to others, be open to what they have to say, but agreeing for the sake of avoiding confrontation will only cause a battle inside yourself, and what is true to you will become foggy. Let go of the people who have let go of you. The only person you need acceptance from is yourself. Uniqueness is very special and is something we have to hold on to, otherwise there will be people who will try to walk all over you. They see your kindness as weakness; don't lie down and let them wipe their dirty feet on you. We are not doormats! Enter the gates of self-love by accepting that not everyone will like you and, hey, you might not like them either. It works both ways. We expect the ones we don't like to accept us, when we would never invite these people around to our homes. So why invite them into your head to eat you up inside? The ones who matter most will flow into your life by adding joyful spirits, and the rest won't matter.

To live a free life, remind your precious self that who you are is who you should always be. Our pride becomes stronger and the confidence we have is at a level where strolling up to a restaurant and saying 'Table for one, please' is no bother. No matter how many friends you have, your best friend will be your own company. Once that taste is there, you will never again let anyone get in between you and the person you are becoming.

Know your worth

Respect yourself enough to walk away from those
who don't give you respect.

Stand up for yourself when you aren't being treated
in the way you deserve.

Know your worth, purely because this is how it should be.

'The person you need is facing you back in the mirror.'

@rewiringthoughts_

Exercise

~~~~~

The three things I love about myself are:

....

....

....

What old beliefs do I need to break free from in order to love myself?

....

....

....

Three new things I will do to help me start accepting who I am:

....

....

....

The start of something new

Her life got stuck in the middle of her days. She didn't know where to look or where to go. All she could think about was who to please and what role to act today. The girl kept playing somebody else until she became exhausted by her own reality. She wanted to wipe the slate clean and start a new beginning, but she did not know where to look. In desperate need of comfort, the girl ran to the mirror, but couldn't recognise who was staring back. All it took was one step closer for the tears to burst out in a panic, mascara streaming down her cheeks, and a desperate roar that demanded an answer from this cruel world: 'WHO AM I?!' Then, long after the eerie pause, a sweet innocent voice whispered back, 'You are who you choose to be.' As she looked in the mirror this time, what appeared was a dominant lioness. Somebody who was ready to take their life back and ready to say "no more" to the suffering that had already been caused. And in that moment, the girl realised that this was the start of something new.

No right, no wrong

'When it comes to a matter of opinion, there is no right or wrong;
it is truly one person's perspective and another's.'

@rewiringthoughts_

I used to believe that there was a right and wrong, but I now realise it's just one human's perspective and another's. The argument that happens over who's right and who's wrong is constant. It divides groups; it causes strain on relationships/friendships, leading some to fall apart. Both accuse the other of their malicious ways while both play the victim, neither one understanding the pain from the other side.

The day I understood, it was clear – everything was a matter of opinion – and from then on I appreciated that. It was a gorgeous summer's day. I was sitting outside feeling the light breeze drift peacefully past me. I felt no worries, no stress; I felt free. Thoughts overflowed from my brain as I meditated and reflected on people's perspectives of one another. 'If I can feel happiness in this present moment, I will feel a sense of freedom. Free from everyone's opinions, including my own.' I don't have to be right or wrong. Neither does anyone else. It is about listening and seeing where your ideas fit into their speech, and vice versa. If you continue to hold your back up and stand firm with anything you say, then maybe some things will feel like an attack, because you are in the habit of thinking there has to be a right and wrong. It's choosing to understand that other people's opinions are just that. We don't have to make everything a battle, so don't take someone's perspective so seriously.

Perspective

The moment my colleagues and I found out we had lost our jobs due to the pandemic, everyone was devastated, worried about what they would do next, but I just couldn't relate. I found it so hard to feel any emotion about it, because that fire in my stomach that I mentioned at the beginning was still there – it just wasn't for this. It sounds crazy, I know, but I was so excited about a new beginning; that's how I saw it. This got me thinking – all of us were told the same information and received the same email, and yet my reaction was: 'I am so excited for my future.' I mean, let's face it, if you heard somebody say those exact words after being told their job is lost and they have bills to pay, I am 99 per cent certain that you would think said person was living on another planet. The truth is that we all store information differently. Our experiences will never be the same, and that's because our perspectives on life are viewed through different lenses which make us so diverse, so distinct from each other.

There's no need to be so stuck in your ways that you can't appreciate a different outlook. It will only isolate you from the people you actually value. It all stems from not being able to have an adult conversation respecting each other's views. Let people think what they want – it's just how they see things at the end of the day. When people want their point to be seen in the limelight, it only makes me hear the sound of children: 'Ha ha, I was right and you weren't – take that!' You see, that little child is the ego talking, and it is our level of awareness that will break us apart from it. Once we recognise the ego for what it is, that is when we will blossom into our true authentic self.

When you take a step back and remove yourself from the situation, you will slowly start to understand somebody else's perspective. Your mind will expand and you will see the bigger picture as you loosen up to conversations, turning them into interesting topics instead of arguments. That's the beauty of perspective – it's knowing that not everything has to involve you and not everything is about you. It's the ego that wants you to believe you are targeted from every angle, which causes you to play the victim or think you are the main star of the show.

It's your perception of what is happening that will make you respond either negatively or positively. Change your perspective and watch it change your life. Try to understand how the other person feels, put yourself in their shoes, and when you do you will start to realise that the things that used to bother you suddenly don't anymore. That's all because you took the "me, myself and I" out of the situation.

Running Free

It's time to let go;

Run off into the sunset.

Free yourself from all the opinions that made you change your
mind about who you are.

Let go of all the storms that have eaten you up inside.

It's time to chase that sunset, my dear.

The ego

Our perspective links to our ego; how we look at life and how we respond to it reflects on our character. For example, if you are comfortable with looking down at others and are obsessed with being right – that's your ego. It loves to be the centre of the universe. There's also another side: you could envy others and ignore the insecurities which your ego tucks deep away. It may have stemmed from childhood experiences, which can cause somebody to have a narcissistic personality, believing it is doing right by protecting us with decisions that transition away from a healthy ego. You have to see everyone as equal human beings.

Ask yourself those questions that dig deep and find the self-doubt which has been hidden for so long. Searching for answers as to why this egotistical front was built up is the first step to knocking the wall down.

The ego that thinks they are better: *'Tell me more gossip about them. I love hearing how they have failed. It makes me feel so much better.'*

The ego that thinks they are worse: *'Why is she getting all the attention and I am not? I get left out all the time.'*

The ego doesn't take responsibility for its lack of awareness. It cannot face the suffering we cause ourselves or the ones around us, nor does it choose to accept it. Bowing down is not an option, because it doesn't want to look secondary. The ego wants to shine in the spotlight, singing, 'Look at me, it's all about me!' or 'I'm losing attention – give me your validation!' The hunger is similar to a spoilt dog crying for more and more food. It is never satisfied; it is always craving. The character the ego makes us play up to is not who we are. Choosing to ignore the false messages that it tries to feed us with will eventually block them from ever taking control.

So how do we break free from it? The only way the ego will get squashed is when you practice your daily awareness. How? By not taking things personally – realising that there is no "you" involved, that there are no sides to take. Recognise the peace in every situation and welcome it with an open heart. Separate yourself from any made-up self-beliefs from the past, knowing they are a habit that only you can break the cycle of. We get so attached to everything; no wonder there are feelings of being attacked by the world.

Think about it. How many times have you taken something the wrong way? Because you believed it was set up for you. 'Urgh, it's always me. Nobody understands!' Now, imagine you got to a place where nothing offended or bothered you. How free would you feel? When we detach ourselves from everything around us – that is when we will let go of the ego. Life becomes enjoyable for what it is rather than just from time to time. If people laugh at you, relax, accept it and smile. If you get soaked by a car as it drives through a puddle, don't take it personally. Tell your friends what happened. They will laugh with you too. That, my friend, is creating a healthy ego.

Start by being totally honest with yourself. If you are always stuck in between arguments, then you have to work on your approach. No beating around the bush – what do you need to do to become a better person in these environments? Once you stop making excuses, start working on your bad habits. That is when you will begin to blossom – isn't that what you want to achieve?

Write your ego a letter – what do you need to do to become your highest self? Remember, honesty is key. Let the ego know you're not getting in role for them today. You are ready for an abundant life, and the way to do this is to be sincere with yourself. The stubborn persona will slowly disappear and watch you walk through life with a confident smile, knowing that nothing can bring you down.

My farewell letter to my ego

Dear Ego,

 I hope you are ready to live a free life just as much as I am. All my life I have chosen to let you win or lose my battles in terms of right or wrong, winner or victim, better or worse. I now realise that there is no right or wrong when sharing our own opinions with others; we shouldn't tear each other down and fight for the limelight to always be right.

 You have always wanted more and more. You are never satisfied, and I am exhausted by this. I didn't pay any attention to my truer self, because I was blinded by your overpowering ways. Pausing in the moment of my prayers, in my breathing, I have come to the conclusion that we were never meant to be.

 I am releasing myself from the prison you have trapped me in. I am ready to live my life by breaking free of the opinions of others and myself. If I hold onto you, I will never become the woman I am destined to be but will have no confidence or self-belief, because you love to compare and separate me from everyone else while you sit there and get a kick out of it.

 Who I am is so much more than who you hold me down to be. Finally I am ready to head towards a destination to find my true self. Entering the world of adventure and self-growth.

 So this gives me the greatest of pleasure to say…

Ego, I am now free.

Yours sincerely, Kate Brownley

Treasuring our peace

It's okay to let go of the person you are now. Don't be afraid that you want to see life through a new lens. Staying in the same place gets boring.

As we get older, we realise we want to live a life of peace and nothing but that.

Once we find our freedom, we keep it locked.

We then remove anyone from our lives who tries to steal that peace we have worked so hard to find.

Change, because you know you deserve to find that unity with yourself.

When you do, I promise you will treasure it for life.

We are all equal

It was a late summer night; the girl decided to go for a walk to the field close by. As she looked up to the sky, the stars were shining one by one, flickering above her. As she began to concentrate deeply, her focus was on counting the stars and picturing them as people. She would spot one glistening from the right, followed by another shining from the left. Then, when she beheld the entire view, she was taken aback by all of the stars shining at different times – almost like a beautiful sequence. It was mesmerising to see them all dazzle individually, a bunch of stars who all appreciated each other for being who they are; that was what the girl needed to see to understand that we humans are all equal.

How you make others feel and how they make you feel should be fuelled with nothing but love. Find the ones who are good for the soul.'

@rewiringthoughts_

Take responsibility for your own actions

'No growth comes from being comfortable.'

@rewiringthoughts_

Taking responsibility for your own actions is knowing that not everyone is against you and that at times the toxicity comes from within. It's understanding that you are not perfect but giving your best efforts to improve builds a foundation which will make these behaviours fizzle out. We all have two different sides to us. There is a side of love, compassion, happiness and consideration, as well as the side of hate, jealousy, anger and resentfulness. The two sides are like heaven and hell, yin and yang. Every morning we have to choose which side to wake up to, just like which side of the bed we get up from. Make the character you strive to be, instead of waiting to see what the day creates for you.

We spoke about the ego which naturally makes us play into the victim mentality; in the same way, taking responsibility for our actions will, in turn, improve our character. I was once that person who didn't take accountability, always getting defensive and in denial of any wrongdoing in a situation. That was the easier option – having my back up against the wall because I thought I was protecting myself. It was the ego who would shout out: 'How dare you accuse me of that?' Then, after the heat from the argument had blown over, I would return like a dog with its tail between its legs to say sorry. Deep down it wasn't sincere – it just naturally flowed out of my mouth to keep the peace; in the process I was hurting others and myself by not owning my shit, not actually caring about what my actions caused – but "sorry" is a word that makes the heart soften. We tend to think that if we say it, it will resolve everything; all actions will be forgotten about. What mattered in these circumstances, however, was that an apology was given. As silly as it feels, it does require courage to do this, and we all have that potential inside of us to make amends, because we don't know how much hurt has been inflicted on another by our behaviour. Having no understanding of the damage we are causing only makes us grow into the identity the ego causes us to play out, forming more toxic ways.

We have to be fully present and pay attention to the way we use our language in these situations. If you apologise just for the sake of it, the person you end up hurting most is yourself, even though you are in denial about it. I'm going to get to the point here: own your stubbornness. How do you know how badly they are hurting inside? A brave face hides the most pain. Understand that speaking in a certain tone will direct which way the conversation will lead; some may still take offence. This quote comes to mind: 'It's not about what you say. It's about how you say it.' We can give the wrong impression by having a distant approach in our tone and body language. If you're having a bad day, don't bring everyone down with you. Instead, let people be aware of your feelings. Be clear; say, 'Hey, I am not feeling myself today.' This will then help those around you have more of an understanding of your current mood, and they can give reassurance that they're available to support you. We are not mind readers, yet there are times when we think others should respect how we feel without openly sharing our emotions. This outlook adds fuel to the flames and only causes frustration.

When you become aware of your toxic behaviour, the process of improving relationships has already begun. Noticing our minor faults when socialising can give the opportunity to maintain a healthy connection. The good news is that you can improve any time you please. You have to want to change for the better, which means you have to "do different". Taking ownership of and responsibility for the words you speak and actions you take will help you knock that wall down. The beauty that comes out of this is that you get put on a path that leads you to the higher road. You start living freely, and isn't this what we all yearn for? A life of freedom.

Two scenarios of victim mentality

'Why me? Why don't I ever win anything? This is just my luck.'

Instead, the mind needs to be empowered by looking at the situation like this:

'I will win next time. I will not give up. I will keep working hard. My time will come when it is meant to be.'

A person with victim mentality feels as if they are being attacked instead of trying to see the lessons in their own actions. The way to improve this mindset is to not let your failures defeat you. Accept what you're not in control of and take responsibility of what you can control, your attitude. Acknowledge that next time you have the chance to create a power shift you will make it happen. No matter how strong the obstacle in the way gets, fight back a thousand times harder. It is about understanding that you have to learn from the setbacks. You will not let them make you feel sorry for yourself. Gift your mind with the courage and confidence to start all over again; it's not a sign of weakness to spot a mistake, but instead is a maturity that people grasp throughout life. Face the music for what it is and don't ignore or cover up with excuses. To change a bad habit is not easy – you have to face your side of anger, envy and resentfulness – but the reward will outweigh all of them combined. No growth comes from being comfortable.

Strip back your identity and work on rebuilding yourself. Do this by getting rid of the pessimistic beliefs you were accustomed to and setting new ones. Lateness is a major common flaw in a lot of us. There is always an excuse, however genuine, for why we don't make the agreed time, but getting defensive over receiving some backlash is the exact mentality we want to avoid. Put it this way: are you ever late to catch a flight for your summer holiday? Extremely rarely. Take ownership of your actions, because if you wanted to be there on time there would be no sugarcoating. Stop blaming other people for your actions and take responsibility. The best gift to ever treat yourself with is to work on yourself. Notice the red flags you send up and remember you have the power to improve yourself in every moment. Which characteristics you want to amplify is your choice. So that leads me to ask you: which character will you choose to be today?

A new version

Don't get caught up in the old version of you.

We are forever changing; be grateful for the person you have been to get you to where you are now.

You may feel that the mask you are hiding beneath makes you superior, but the person you aren't showing is worth so much more than who you settle for.

Show the world who you really are.

This new version of you

Is what the world wants to see.

It was time for a change

She was always so angry at the world, pointing the finger at everyone else, until one day she heard her next-door neighbour through the wall, playing the flute. Her whole body became relaxed; she couldn't help but smile brightly. The calming notes made her mind drift off to a tropical summer's day, running along the beach with the sand between her toes. The smell of the ocean, the heat on the skin, taking the girl off into a world of her own until…the flute stopped. Her eyes opened; inside she felt no anger, just pure love. She couldn't help but question: was this a consequence? Or was it fate? But the gift from the little girl next door made her realise it was time for a change.

'You have to understand that not everyone is against you and the toxicity comes from yourself.'

@rewiringthoughts_

Set yourself some boundaries

'Make yourself the main priority.'

@rewiringthoughts_

Have you ever said yes to a plan then immediately afterwards thought, 'Oh shit, how am I going to talk myself out of this one?', but felt too guilty to say no? I used to always put others before myself, which burned up my energy to do anything for me. I was your typical yes girl. 'Cup of tea at my house, Kate?' 'Yes!' I would force out. 'Night out next week, Kate?' 'Sure thing!' 'I need you to come tonight to give me some advice. Is that okay, Kate?' 'YES!!' Sometimes I question whether I even let people finish their sentences before I agreed. If I didn't verbally, I already had in my mind. The word "yes" became more common than a morning cuppa; better yet, I was agreeing to unnecessary things before even having a sip! You could sit on my head ten times and spin me backwards twice and I would still allow it. Anything to please others, because I thought that's what being a good person was. To put others before myself was something that came naturally to me. It became almost robotic, without considering whether I really wanted to do it. This made me unable to recognise what some may see as too much of an effort. I lost myself in the process of wanting to please others and never stopped to ask, 'What direction do I want to go in?', or a simple 'How are you today, Kate?' There was no time to face my emotions head on. Friends and family would phone for advice, which would make me answer in the middle of a meal just to take the call. I felt too guilty to ignore anyone because

I had no boundaries set in place – and that was the real problem.

Why is it we dive into other people's swimming pools, drowning ourselves in their worries? We act as if our feelings aren't valid or are not good enough to receive tender loving care. Is it because we find it so hard to say no? Do we struggle with letting someone down and so neglect our own self-care? Seriously, let that one sink in. If you are saying yes to everyone else, that means you are saying no to yourself. Boundaries are something that can help you manage this – you are still supplying kindness while having energy to focus on your own needs. If you don't have any set, then the robot life will begin to take over. You will be drained from the requests and stuck on autopilot. Being everyone else's knight in shining armour is great, but when you have enough on your plate, dealing with what's going on inside you will get buried deep for another day. Think of it as being a superhero: you have two separate identities. One is prepared to be there for the world, and the other lives a private life. Deal with your problems first! Your mental health should be the main priority. I am not saying other people's feelings aren't important, because they are, but if you aren't healed then how can you heal another person?

Grow into the person you want to become instead of keeping up with everyone else's life more than your own – as if they are the Kardashians and you are their viewer. You will become mentally exhausted if you watch the same episodes when you know there's a series inside you waiting to be viewed. If you're finding yourself involved in other people's mess then you need to take a step back. Stop giving to the ones who don't appreciate it or respect you. I had to become so down and exhausted for that moment to come around for me. Ready for a change, I grabbed the nearest pen and paper and off I began to go into self-discovery. At first it was a long stare down at a blank piece of paper, not knowing where to begin, but all it took was a bit of concentration and all my thoughts would suddenly flush out like water from a burst pipe! I had a chapter of this book locked up inside me, waiting to be released.

There were my feelings in black and white – goals jotted down and a clear vision for what was next. I had to be lost in order to be found. Time alone was what I needed to make my inner voice louder without any distractions from others. The taste of freedom had never felt better, and all I needed to do to get that was to say no. It will have a significant positive spin on your life. You and your soul will reunite; that self-growth will become addictive.

Some of you could be thinking: 'Well, does that mean I should turn down a job opportunity?' Absolutely not. Say yes to every chance which will make you grow mentally, spiritually and financially, but when it comes to putting yourself first, learn to give a good no. It doesn't have to be an aggressive rejection – speak your words gracefully. Life is way too short to be wasting your time on people and situations that won't make you develop, so don't feel guilty about that. Young and naïve, we spend our days with the wrong crowd, unknowingly doing things that waste our precious time. Then we get to 21, and after that every birthday comes around at a pace we can't slow down. The panic of life begins: there are things we have always wanted to do, and realisation hits hard that time is ticking, so we cherish it and put ourselves first. Nobody lives your life for you and this is why you have to value time. Make choices that please you, because it is never selfish living a life that makes you happy. On the flip side, remember to also respect others' wishes of wanting to be alone; it works both ways. We need to normalise setting boundaries for our well-being.

I want to remind you about the benefits of slowing down and prioritising yourself. Treat your body as if it were charging a mobile phone overnight so it can be 100 per cent ready and prepared for the next day. When switching off from the world, you claim back your life, and that is time that is never lost. The power in saying no will teach you: in order to heal, be prepared to let someone down. That way you can give greater service to those who need it. What else is important is finding the balance! Not all of the things you agree to will suit your needs, because at those times you will want to help the people close to you, but finding the balance will filter out the unnecessary requests, which you should feel no shame in rejecting. Remember, you don't have to answer everyone when you aren't feeling up to it. It's okay to go quiet and disappear until you feel like you again. Take a day off, put yourself on 'charge' and be surprised at what you will discover in silence.

Discovered

During time alone in silence,

She discovered her inner voice,

Telling her, 'Don't be scared to let go of people.'

When you grow, you lose friends.

Working on yourself is what will plant and harvest the
breakthrough that is around the corner.

Which is more important – chasing your dreams or helping
somebody else make theirs come true?

It's okay to disappear

When it all got a bit too much, she withdrew into her own world. As the sun set, shining through her window, it reminded her that the sun doesn't shine all day either. It has its moments when it hides away from the rest of the world and goes missing for a bit, just like her. For the sun to shine at its brightest it needs time alone in quietness to reflect and collect its thoughts. Sometimes the best journeys start from hiding for a little while until you feel whole again, and that's okay. Then you will be ready for your comeback, to shine brighter.

It's okay to disappear, my love.

'It's okay to switch off from the world and go missing until you feel better. Take as long as you need.'

@rewiringthoughts_

Exercise: set yourself new boundaries

What will you change in order to create new boundaries for yourself?

....

....

....

What do you need to do to make sure you recharge?

....

....

....

What do you need to say no to in order to make yourself a priority?

....

....

....

Create a morning and evening schedule

'Dedicate this next month to yourself.'

@rewiringthoughts_

I was the girl who loved to sleep. It took priority over waking up early in the morning and getting stuff done. I thought I needed ten hours (twelve after a long day). Anything less than eight hours and I would panic inside, thinking, 'This is not enough', and 'I won't be at my best for the day'. Every time that dreadful sound on my alarm clock went off it made me feel as if I was being woken up by the sound of nails scratching a blackboard. Urgh, it was so painful. It always made my skin crawl. I hit that snooze button out of habit, jumping back into bed, thinking, 'If only I could stay here all day.' I was lazy and that's how it was – no excuses.

My family knew most how much I idolised sleep. After recently moving out, I quickly found out that it is your own responsibility to get up and motivate yourself. There is no one to force you to wake up and tell you it's a beautiful day ahead. At first I thought it was great – I could stay in bed all day without being told off – but when it actually came to it, the overwhelming feeling of guilt reigned over me, and it was far worse than any alarm clock I had ever heard. I set myself a commitment to wake up early the next day and start my writing.

The morning arrived and that wretched noise began to ring in my ears. 6am. The feeling of it being the first day back at school all over again. Two distinct voices in my head were like five-year-olds, fighting over who gets the Barbie doll. One voice saying, 'I am not getting up, I am so comfy', while the other screams, 'Move yourself right now!' The obvious truth was that I already wanted to throw the towel in and jump back into bed. As I sat there debating what to do, I realised that the whining voice in my head was not someone I wanted to be. That was enough motivation to pick myself up and seize the day ahead. I didn't want to be that person ever again. The feeling of *I am actually doing this* while brushing my teeth and looking in the mirror was great. The productivity was rushing through me, and I hadn't even started. What an achievement for the girl who would sleep all day if she could. After a successful trial run, I continued to have a 6am start, this time with morning stretches and a relaxing shower while playing the empowering and timeless classic 'Man! I Feel Like A Woman!' by Shania Twain. In that split second of getting ready before the sun had barely risen, let me tell you, I felt invincible. My mornings for that next month were incredible, because each time I kept upgrading my routine with a little bit extra. For example, I gave myself mini pep talks in the mirror before I headed out, got the blood pumping with a 'dance like nobody is watching' vibe. By the end, it was pretty much the scene from *Matilda* where her energy lifted the entire surroundings. I had perfected it.

The next question is how to put that energy towards something worthwhile. For me, the answer was easy. In order to become the author I am destined to be, to reach out to as many people as possible and make them see their worth, I journalled, so that one day I could turn it into a book. Mornings and evenings were my only realistic slots, i.e. before and after work, but, because I loved it and had this encouragement from my routine, I treated it as my gift for the day. The laptop would open and off my fingers went, typing and writing as I kept my reasons at the forefront of my mind. Who would've thought that getting up early would make me feel so rewarded? The best time to make a start on your goals is of a morning, as your productivity is much higher. The early starts turned into my 'precious time'.

We choose to run downstairs excitedly on Christmas morning, palms sweating, hands shaking with excitement for what we're about to receive. So, what if we choose to think and believe Christmas Day is every day, that life is a gift wrapped under the tree every morning? Our mindset can determine whether we walk down the stairs miserably for the other 364 days of the year, or we can wake up excited – grateful for what lies ahead. Think about it: when you go on holiday, do you walk around with a spring in your step? This is because you find a reason to get up and enjoy the holiday. Now think of that as your day-to-day life, whether that is scheduling a workout, reading a few pages of a book, or simply doing the things you get fulfilment from. Find the time to do what your heart desires. Do something today that can change your tomorrow. Make that start, no matter how small it is, and observe progression. Even just getting out of bed and applying for a few jobs – that's still progress. My comfort zone was my bed; I am pretty sure it's most people's, right? As you push yourself out of your comfort zone, that's when you transform.

Routines bring discomfort at first; that's why I challenge you to take time out to create one. Schedule in your diary the things that bring fulfilment to you, then create a realistic slot for when you are going to do them. Treat the first few times as trials and keep working at it until it becomes second nature. Then move onto the next. Never stop learning! Find the balance as well as mixing up each routine to keep it fun, and watch productivity in your life excel.

Growth

You will amaze yourself

When you do the things you never thought were possible.

The ideas you dreamed of that were 'too big' now become a reality.

Because you made it happen.

I guess that's what makes us – doing more and being more.

Always finding ourselves through each struggle.

To me, that's why we should always choose growth.

Motivation

If you are reading this now and thinking, 'If only she worked my job, she would understand', I get it. Your day job deflates the life and soul out of you every single time you enter the building. You clock-watch for the entire day, waiting for it to strike five o'clock. You can't stand your boss, who always adds extra tension on top of your day, and you feel there is no way out. Each day consists of daydreaming of that next holiday or that moment you finally win the lottery and become a millionaire so you can walk out, never to work again. However, the reality is that you're becoming comfortable at settling for less instead of pushing yourself out of the lazy zone, when you're much more capable than you believe.

Motivation: where does it come from? Does Tinker Bell really travel to your house and sweep you off your feet to Neverland, and you return suddenly motivated? Well, let me burst that bubble for you and make it clear: there is no such thing. If you are waiting for the day Tinker Bell kidnaps you then you will be looking out of the window for the rest of your life. Motivation isn't something that gets brought to you like a parcel – you have to make it happen. Think of it as a magic trick. It's not as simple as the magician just saying 'Abracadabra' and it's done. They have to plan and prepare long before the fancy five-syllable word, and find that motivation daily to trust that the performance will be as great as when it first came into their head. The magician's motivation made you believe in magic. The same goes for you. That magic is already inside there; the key is to not let it slip every time it comes around. Every time you do something, ask yourself: what is my reason behind this? Let those reasons motivate you. If you are eating fruit, ask yourself: what is my reason? Is it to get healthier? That is your motivation to get to that magic point where you can say 'Abracadabra' too. Your whys and reasons will guide you to where you are destined to be. I had days when writing this book gave me head fog, and I wanted to call it a day there and then. I reminded myself why by envisioning the end product – people getting fulfilment from reading my book.

If you don't work on taking the time to question your actions and reasons, then you will become unstuck. Alarm clocks aren't fun, trying to figure out shit isn't easy, and that first step is always the hardest – but it is also the greatest. It's the beginning of something new, even if you have gone back to it. It takes courage to pick up where you last left off. If your body or mind is tired and needs a rest, listen to it. Take a break; just don't quit! Get an early night and start all over again tomorrow. Never give up on something that made you feel in the first place. The moment you want to give up is a sign to keep going. Why? Because when a breakthrough is just round the corner, so many people call it a day right before their time comes. The more you work through the uncertainty, the more the answers come to the surface.

Whatever you are working towards is there for the taking – believe that. If you dedicate two hours in the morning to the things you love, this gains you 14 hours a week extra, which adds up to 56 hours in a month, 672 hours in a year. What does this tell us? Time is not lost if it can be gained. Be consistent and you will soon see that results come from taking action and being self-disciplined. Acknowledge your lazy habits every time they come around – just get up, and let that kickstart the process for you. Sooner or later you will have to make the first move and start, so why not go for it now?

Take baby steps

We put so much pressure on ourselves to have everything completed. We want things done there and then, and if it's not finished within a time frame we become frustrated, setting ourselves up for failure by rushing. This is why taking baby steps and completing small tasks will feel more rewarding – because they appear easier to achieve, when really you are doing the same amount of work. They are little boosts of motivation which keep you going rather than draining you. I am not saying don't set yearly goals – please do – but break them down into little pieces instead of putting pressure on yourself to do the entire mission. This way you won't lose interest by the time the deadline arrives. Some people quit if it hasn't happened over a fortnight, and it's no wonder, because they rush instead of slowing down and enjoying the process. When you set yourself realistic goals, they will make you much more motivated than cramming a whole project onto your hands, believe me.

Paint one stair at a time each day, not the whole lot, and before you know it you have completed the staircase. It will take longer but it will be done properly. Your consistency and self-discipline will get you to your destination in style. It's the small moves we make daily that have the biggest impact on us as they add up. All you need to do is focus on putting one foot in front of the other. Time is not against you; there is no rush. The great Wall of China took 2,000 years to build, it didn't happen overnight – let that one sink in.

One day at a time

Stop putting a deadline on the tasks you feel need to be done.

Trust that it is all going to happen.

Let it flow and watch it all unfold beautifully for you.

Do your best in everything you do, because that will always be enough.

Take it one day at a time and I promise

You will get there.

Evening routine

It took me a while to understand how important an evening routine was. When 10pm came, I turned into a night owl. From 1am till 2am, tossing and turning was the routine for me most nights. The brain couldn't function the next day. Overworking and burning myself out through meaningless things like scrolling on Instagram and texting until all hours – it really wasn't healthy. No wonder that when it came to the morning, I wanted to sleep in. When I had to force myself up, headaches became more common. They were worse than any hangover, and that was saying something.

Our phones get in the way of our daily routines; they are the biggest distractions. Once we finish a hard day's work, we come home to the socially accepted pattern of using our phones or sitting on the couch, binge-watching as relaxation. Of course, it's absolutely fine to do these things, but with balance. Some people finish work in the evening around 5pm but treat their free time unproductively, when in reality there is a time slot of five to six hours to do whatever you please. Granted, some may have responsibilities within this timeframe like cooking and caring for their children, but there will still be time to dedicate to yourself. Even if it's 20 minutes you can make the best use of this slot by unwinding, whether that be by catching up on a TV show while preparing your meal or simply calling a friend to chat. Then you can choose to do the hobbies that you get fulfilment from. Maybe practising an instrument, or having a hot bath with your favourite book, or even simply walking your favourite route. These things that amuse us so easily are what release our dopamine hormone and make life in general better. When it comes to the latter half of the evening, prepare for the day ahead by laying out the clothes you will wear or writing a to-do list of those things that need to be done. Then you can go back to relaxing, but this time replace the phone with a book, and the TV with the sound of sleep meditation. This will calm your body just in time for bed. To get our sleep under control, we have to make sure we switch off at least an hour or two before bed; that goes for all electronic devices. Otherwise you will have that one song you listened to playing over and over in your head until 3am. It makes me question: when did we lose the tolerance for curfews from our parents? At what point did we let routine slip out of our hands?

Get organised

Working a full-time job as well as keeping up with house chores and writing a book, I found it extremely difficult to keep on top of myself by following a routine. The stress of juggling them all together became too much. I had no plans set in place for each day, so it wasn't a surprise that simple tasks were not always completed. I had no structure or clear vision of what my days would consist of, because of lack of organisation. Every time a thought appeared in my head, I would convince myself to remember it in the morning; but when the day arrived, guess what? I forgot! A cluttered lifestyle actually left me with more work to do, because I was having to pick up on things that should have already been nipped in the bud, rather than allocating time to duties. If you wanted to get your hair done you would phone up and book an appointment, right? The same goes for things on the to-do list. We need to give ourselves appointments to do house chores, to see family and friends and to work on our goals.

Although organisation should be included for stability, we don't want it to control every aspect of our life, otherwise where is the excitement in the unexpected? It will, in fact, have the opposite effect and ruin your mood, because it hasn't followed your schedule. Prioritise what needs to be arranged most importantly and let the rest go with the wind. For example, you could have scheduled for this afternoon that you are finally going to paint the fence, but all of a sudden your family come round to ask if you want to go for a meal. Because you're so enticed by the schedule you created, it feels almost like a disturbance to what was originally planned. When we see it from a distant point of view, however, the obvious choice is to pick your family every time. You organise to help what's going on in your life, not to direct it.

Once you get into the habit of a routine, notice the benefits that come with it. You will be on your A game – and who doesn't want to feel like they have their shit together? Every time you miss something on the list, or forget to even write one, you will instantly be reminded of the hectic life that once was, and will feel compelled to never go back there again. Give yourself a minute to create a morning/evening timetable. Include a section for some "me time", and the rest is history.

Declutter belongings

It may be that it's not your schedules that need organising but your surroundings. Is your home messy? Do you make your bed in the morning? These minor comforts, however small you think they are, can vastly improve your mindset. When living at home, I didn't value my room, nor did I think that cleaning made a difference to whether or not I had a clear focus. I kept so many tangible objects for memories – even clothes from when I was fifteen years old! I know, I know. Bin those clothes immediately. Well, the great news is: I did. I reached a point where my space (or lack of it) was irritating the life out of me, like a rash on the skin.

I decided enough was enough; being tidy was a new goal I set for myself, and it started with making the bed as soon as I rose out of it. After that, I began to remove all unnecessary items – things that didn't bring any purpose to my life – and that got the ball rolling, all from making sure my bed covers looked neat. They say 'messy bed, messy head', and I couldn't agree more.

Think about it. How satisfying is it to see your bed made neatly? The comparison of how the beds are is a reflection of your mood at the beginning of the day. Our surroundings play such a huge role in our mentality and that is why keeping your home tidy and organised is key to a healthier lifestyle. Reorganise your belongings and watch it reorganise your life. It is out of habit we cling to objects that don't resonate with us, because we want to remember them as we found or experienced with them. Don't leave the clutter or it will have an effect on you. Messy surroundings, messy head, indeed.

Let tomorrow be the day when you realise how easy it is to change. Make that bed! Throw out junk that serves no purpose. Clean that workstation you haven't cleaned in months and watch performance grow. Create space in your surroundings and leave room for all the magnificent ideas to come through. Being untidy will never again become an option for you.

Do better

Sometimes it feels like too much effort to "do different",

Maybe because being where we are feels pretty comfy. But the truth is, we can all improve our well-being.

We just have to try, not to impress anybody, but because life's all about outgrowing yesterday's version of us.

You owe it to yourself to become the best you can be.

Get up today and do better, my love. I promise you can.

Realisation

As the girl went to pick some flowers in between the fields, everywhere felt super open. She felt so comfortable and wished only for her home to be like this; each flower had its own space. As the girl picked the daffodils one by one, something clicked. She shot up, ran back to her little cottage, full of inspiration, and told herself, 'If these fields could clear my mind by every flower having its own space, then I can recreate that in my home and feel like this.' The girl started to throw away all the junk. Each sweep was making her heart beat faster as she started to see her bedroom floor. The adrenalin was pumping through her whole body as she started to understand that cleaning her surroundings would improve her mindset. She had been living in a home that brought her so much sadness. The girl thanked those fields of flowers that day, and the only things she made room for were the daffodils, which reminded her why she had been compelled to make a start in the first place.

'Nothing will happen if you don't start.'

It was a blessing in disguise

'Through the darkness you will find your strength.'

@rewiringthoughts_

It was February 2019. A group of us went skiing in Alpe d'Huez, in France. I had had lessons the year before back at home and over in France at our last skiing resort. This year, I felt it in my bones: I was ready, baby! I felt confident and so excited to get back on the slopes. Well, apart from those deadly black slopes. They looked deadly to me, because I was still new to the party. If you haven't been skiing before, I will give you an insight as to what each slope is. You start with the beginners' slopes, which are green, then it's blue, red and then black. Our trip was for six days, and every day was a red-slope day. It was so exhausting for me as the rest of the group were pros at skiing. They would amaze me every day with their talent and speed. A red slope felt like a green to them, and the red slopes felt like the blacks to me. I most definitely kept them all waiting; but, of course, I was worth the wait.

It was day six, Friday 8 February 2019, around 3pm – a moment that changed my life forever. It was our final day of skiing and we had just finished for lunch. I said to the group, 'I will meet you all at the bar by our resort. I am calling it a trip. I'm done.' The universe must have overheard me and thought, 'You're not done with me just yet, missus.' The sun was shining on the slopes. It was so challenging to keep my balance as the slope was thin and icy. I took my time and kept telling myself, 'You're nearly there, Kate. A glass of wine is your command when you get to the bottom.'

Then, as I came onto the next slope, it was using up so much of my energy that my whole body and legs had already decided to call it a day. As I came down the slope a snowball of ice was falling. Seconds before it reached me, I gripped my sticks with my sweaty gloves, trying to stop myself from falling. Was it fate? Who knows? The snowball dropped in front of me and I lost all control. As I went over, my right ski came off automatically, but my left ski was still attached as I fell down the mountain. I panicked as I tried to see through my steamy goggles, praying I would land safely. Landing off-piste in a pile of snow saved my life that day. If I had fallen left, I would have fallen off the Alpe d'Huez mountains, 2,000 metres up, and I am 100 per cent certain that if that had happened I wouldn't be writing a book or sharing my story with you now.

As I sat there trying to move my leg, I knew something was up. The pain was like nothing I had ever experienced before. I was in shock. I didn't want to be a nuisance to the rest of the group, so I tried to mask it by treating it as a "little fall", but as soon as I attempted to get up, I knew it was far worse than that. The discomfort and irritation in my leg was increasing at such a rapid pace it was making my whole body twitch. I downplayed the whole situation, and the funny thing is that the group all got me down the mountain. Yes, I came down the mountain sitting on my arse. I had some of the group manoeuvre me down on their snowboards. One even skied backwards while I held the ski sticks for control as it was so steep, and the rest of the group was the traffic patrol police, guiding the traffic. It was a crazy sight to say the least. Two hours later we had made it down the mountain. The pain was coming on aggressively in my left leg; thank God there was an ambulance ready to take me to the hospital. Finally, I was seen by a doctor. He said, 'Remove your ski trousers and let's have a look.' I tried to move but the pain was unbearable. Two doctors helped me remove my baggy trousers. Underneath I had my skintight leggings on. As I looked at my leg I felt dizzy. I tilted my head back, my hands went lifeless and my eyes were flashing. I was so close to passing out.

It's a good job they didn't have mirrors in that room, because if I had looked at my leg from other angles I would have been out like a light. It was swollen like a balloon and the knee pointed in another direction. Even typing this now, my arms go weak as I am taken right back to that horrid event. I had never experienced a break in my body while growing up, and this was most definitely a huge scare.

One of the doctors looked at my knee. I didn't understand her as she was French, but I think she said something along the lines of 'Shit'; that's what it felt like, anyway. I was screaming that in my head, that's for sure! They say an average person has 50,000 to 60,000 thoughts a day. I reckon mine tripled that. Sitting on the bed, gazing at the wall, I couldn't help but picture me walking down the aisle getting married in the future with a wooden leg. My mind couldn't help but run wild with negative thoughts. I was due to be starting my new beauty job for a different brand in just five days! My mind was thinking, 'Just my luck, hey?' I then snapped myself out of it and repeated my famous words, 'It is what it is,' as I prepared myself for the worst. I was ready to accept what was coming my way; and at the end of the day I was still alive, and that was what mattered the most.

The staff ran off to bring in another doctor. He checked over my leg and said, 'Miss Brownley, it's not good. We need to save your leg as the blood is all joined in your top thigh.' I mean, what was I supposed to do when he said those words with so much panic – run away? I don't think that was on the cards for me. The doctors injected me with all sorts and I still managed to keep calm. Even though my calf was black and blue, I knew this was not the time for me to say goodbye to my leg; it was not possible! As I lay there on the hospital bed, I closed my eyes and imagined myself running with my future children, and there I was walking down the aisle; and in that moment I knew my leg wasn't going anywhere.

Not long after the doctor came back in, he dragged a stool over and sat beside me. I had to be the first to get my words out, as I couldn't wait any longer for an answer! I asked, 'Will I lose my leg?' He laughed and looked me straight in the eye and said, 'No, you won't lose your leg. It is still very serious, and you will need to be seen to straight away when you are home.' I shouted out loud: 'THANK YOU, THANK YOU!'

The doctor looked at me with concern. He didn't have to tell me he thought I was crazy, because it was written all over his face. I didn't have any questions for him, nor did I have a care in the world for what was coming. I had been ready for them to take my leg off. To then be told my leg was saved – I couldn't help but feel like I had been lucky, and it was a feeling I will never forget. My whole left leg got bandaged up, I got my crutches and off we went. Heading home for a new adventure. If only I had known what was in store for me.

For the first few weeks I handled my recovery process like a trouper, upbeat and positive every day. It felt like a walk in the park. Too good to be true? Then one day I hit a brick wall. In week 5 of my injury, I was told I would be off work for another four to five months. It hit me so hard I felt at an all-time low. I was depressed; it was a gigantic pill to swallow and I couldn't accept it. I was crying myself to sleep in the evening; angry, sad – you name it, I felt it. I was exhausted at having no independence and putting on a brave face for the last five weeks.

In week 6 I slowly learned how to get my left leg walking again. It took up every single part of my energy, and the pain had caused me to sink into depression. I felt nothing but anxiety every day. It got especially bad in the evening. Sick to death of looking at my bedroom ceiling and using my crutches, I just wanted to walk again. It made me realise how important all the small things in life are. I missed being able to drive, get a shower and even run down the stairs in 0.5 seconds for a chocolate biscuit. Most importantly, I missed being able to walk on my two feet. It sucked. Sleepless nights and repeating the daily exercises became physically and mentally draining. Added to all this, I needed to get back to work for the money to pay my bills. Missing out on so many parties and social events had sunk me deeply into victim mentality.

I was depressed. I really was at rock bottom; I couldn't have been any lower if I had tried. Distraught from the inside out, I had no hope for life. The depression came out of nowhere and only left me feeling empty and numb inside. I was stuck in the mindset of thinking it wouldn't get better, when the truth is, it always does. And then one morning I woke up with the warmth of the sun on my cheeks. It felt as though heaven had come knocking on my door. I smiled with so much passion because I knew this was a new day with a clear path to step forward on. I told myself I would not go back to the place I had been in and that I had the power to change this. After getting myself back into my books and reading, I felt more "me" than ever before. Nothing could stop me; I was unbreakable. The injury wasn't my fault, but my attitude towards the healing was my responsibility. Something that was so traumatic turned out to be the most beautiful self-growing experience. My injury had given me time not only to rest my leg but to rest my mind. It taught me I could recreate my life and myself from scratch. I was journalling my thoughts every day, focusing on my bad habits and asking myself, 'How can I improve?' Every day from that day onwards was like my first day back at school, learning how to become the best version of me. I became obsessed with self-growth.

When the day came around when I had to return to work, I went back to life as a completely different person from before. I put myself at the top of my list, and everyone else was below that. My self-love was stronger than ever before and nobody could break me this time. I chose myself. The secret to breaking free from this is to realise that you are your own ticket out of this mess! No matter how hopeless you feel, when you decide to make a stop to this hopelessness is when your life changes for the better. No matter how bad your experience was, no matter how painful your scars are, your response to it is what plays the biggest role. If you don't make it an easy ride for yourself, you will have to live with the pain you have fuelled on top. Don't choose to be the victim – don't let this destroy you. Your pain is temporary but your memories are permanent, and this is why I ask you to use your time wisely. Read more books, work on your mindset and let this be your "soul-searching time". This moment will not come back around again – the universe won't stop the clock just for you – so use it wisely. Don't let the trauma traumatise you. Recreate your journey so that when you look back in a year's time you will be so proud of how you handled it all. The growth lies in your perspective of it all. We have to trust and remember that it will get better – nobody stays at the top of a rollercoaster for the whole duration of the ride. You have to come down, up and all around; the same goes for life.

I ask you to let my words guide you, let them give you the confidence boost that you need to get moving. If I got through six months of pain then so can you, my friend. Take this opportunity with both hands and make the best out of a shitty situation. This positive attitude will give you a story to tell to inspire others, and when you share it you will show them that the beauty of being in the dark is that it always brings you to search for the light. Through the darkness you found your strength and you made it out of your recovery. Then one day you are walking through the park, you find a bench, and as you sit on it you glance up to the sky, see the clouds that pass you by and you smile, because it was all a blessing in disguise.

Stronger

~~~

You had to fall so deep to get woken up from this daydream you were living in.

Your breakdown turned into the making of you.

Finally you saw the strength you held inside. As soon as life hit hard, you got up and bounced back stronger.

Unknown

Throw yourself into every challenge you face no matter how painful it feels. Now is the time to step outside your comfort zone. You haven't got anything to lose other than the feeling of regret if you don't try. Nothing in this world will hurt more than knowing you didn't put your whole heart into something. Give yourself a shot, because if you don't, there will always be a part of you that repeats the words "what if" in your head, wondering where your life would be if you had done differently.

It's time to be strong, my dear, and step into the unknown. Let today be the day you make your first step. I promise, you will blossom like never before and there is not a greater feeling than outgrowing your old self.

Future self; I am coming for you.

You have all the answers inside

'Energy is there for a reason. Pay attention to how you feel. Listen to your gut. It will tell you everything you need to know. Trust it.'

@rewiringthoughts_

Intuition is when you pick up on a feeling about a person or situation beyond rational reasoning. It is called a gut feeling and it took me many years to understand why this sixth sense emerges. You could describe it as being almost like a swirling kick to the stomach, which I initially believed was nerves. Now I understand it is a sign of direction. Your future self is attempting to wake you the hell up before it unfolds! It screams: 'Pay attention to me. I am here for a reason, which is to help you figure out your true, authentic self.'

In the middle of recovery from my knee injury, I raised the question, 'Am I happy with the life I have? What do I want to do and who do I want to become?' Every day a random thought would appear in my brain, never leaving me. It was like the mini tribe of the family from *The Borrowers* trying to offload questions, as if they had camped in either ear, screenplaying scenarios of me in another role, expressing little snippets and tasters of what could be my future. They wouldn't stop until I gave my full attention to their concerns, pushing me to question their very existence in my mind. One night I couldn't shift the vision out of my head. The family came knocking on my temples, shouting, 'Wakey, wakey! You're not getting away with ignoring your true purpose that easily!' I woke up from my half-slumber and it was 1:05am. I was confused from the vision that kept revisiting my mind. As I sat with these thoughts that had built up over time, they begged a final question: 'Why can't I stop dreaming of this random book?' The Borrowers were trying to get me to think of my future self, but I couldn't quite grasp the message – until now. Out came my journal and I jotted down "Holding a book", leaving it as that without understanding the real purpose of where it came from. (FYI, I didn't really think the Borrowers were in my head.)

Your passion is deep inside

I struggled to find the meaning after that. It wasn't something that just clicked overnight, because I never imagined myself to be writing a book. I thought it was just that I have a love of reading and that's why it came into my head, the same as listening to music. I tried to believe it was for a deeper meaning, but can you have a talent for reading? To see other people so fulfilled from knowing the path they were on made me feel like a failure at life. I couldn't help but feel so empty inside, and was struggling to come to terms with there not being a simple solution to finding my very own path. The thought of living a free life and doing what I loved felt so far away – impossible, in fact! It was a feeling of being disconnected from everything around me.

A moment passed with my head in my hands, pressing onto the side of my temples, searching for answers. As I closed my eyes I went into a daze, massaging the pain to release the confusion that was mounting up inside me. As I focused deeper, the hurt faded, cast away by the healing powers of the tips of my fingers. I saw a light. As I looked closer, I saw the same book! In my vision I grabbed it with both hands and, when flicking through the pages, something extraordinary happened. For the first time in my life I saw my pathway laid out. It was crystal clear to me that...the book was mine! I jumped out of my chair and screamed out loud: 'WHAT THE HELL? THIS IS A SIGN! THIS IS A SIGN!!'

I had been so oblivious, but, thinking back, it was the lack of confidence that had blinded me. I grabbed my journal and there they were, the words staring back at me: 'Holding a book.' With goosebumps all over my body, I cried so many happy tears. It most definitely felt as though the Borrowers family had come back, this time with their scissors, as they cut the wires in my head and set me free. They meant business! The relief! My memory took me back, revisiting all the patterns I was doing daily. The notes written in my phone were preparing me for this book. Subconsciously I was doing the work but failing to see the signs, because I wasn't present enough. But I knew that fire in my belly was always there, and this was confirmation to pursue something great. It was the closest I have ever got to feeling that burning sensation which smouldered within me. Patience was all I needed for my passion to catch up from my heart to my head.

We frustrate ourselves, thinking all the answers are there in plain sight, but if you trust the choices you make then this builds a spellbinding bond with your intuition. Your gut knows before you do; that is intuition talking. It is always signalling something when you don't have the clear answers. Stop searching and look within, because everything you need is there. Pay attention to what your body tells you – I can guarantee something in your day holds the sign of your true passion; it's just that your awareness of it isn't there. To avoid distractions, don't pretend to be somebody you're not. That will only get you to a destination which doesn't align with your authentic life purpose, and will block your potential.

This is a process you have to experience; and when that moment arrives, be thankful. When you start paying attention to what's going on inside, you will connect all the dots together. Never having to worry about your future or what's to come, because you know it will all work out, just like it's supposed to. Trust more, my dear, trust. Remember, if you haven't figured out what you want to do yet then that's okay. The penny always drops when you least expect it. You could be eating your cereal and then all of a sudden the uncertainty you had about life disappears. Just like that, it all makes sense when you least expect it! Your passion comes through to the surface of your thoughts on a random Thursday morning. The answers you searched for come to you right there, as they were already within.

Listen to that feeling you get in your gut; let it guide you. It is your own personal satnav – trust the route it wants to take you on.

Finding you

Life has a funny way of directing us into our paths.

When it gets confusing, don't overthink it.

Trust what happens.

Trust me when I say this:

What is for you will never pass you by,

And what is yours will always find you.

'I guess the most heartbreaking thing is experiencing something that you never thought would happen. Starting a new life that you never set out to do. But we have to trust how we feel and let our intuition guide us or we will never know what life has in store for us.'

@rewiringthoughts_

She believed she could, so she did

Isn't it funny how some memories we can't revisit and some stick, taking us back to them as if it were yesterday? As I mentioned, school was a chore. To make it even worse, I didn't do very well, as I daydreamed about dance all day long. The only class I ever really enjoyed was English. One day, as I was heading for an exam, a teacher wished everyone else good luck, then turned to me and said, 'Pigs will be able to fly before you pass your exams, Katie.' I remember nervously laughing with a short response: 'Thanks.' I was fifteen, already hating school, and to make me despise it even more, that teacher put the cherry on top of the cake. I entered the exam a bag of nerves, feeling worse than I had before. That teacher's words hit deep. For the last eleven and a half years, they have never left my mind. They fuelled my drive to prove them wrong, for sure. I wouldn't want to share the name of the teacher who said those words to me, because deep down I actually liked her. Maybe her words inspired me to achieve. But if you are reading my book, teacher of my past, I would like to let you know... Pigs are still not flying, but I am.

I believed I could, so I did.

Something sparked inside

When that teacher told her pigs would be able to fly before she could ever achieve anything, it happened to spark something inside her. It made her stand up for herself when nobody else would. It made her believe in herself more than anyone else ever could. Making the girl fight for what she wanted in life, on the hunt for finding her purpose. Every challenge she came across didn't make her stop – it pushed her to do more. She wanted to prove a point to that teacher and herself. The girl knew from that day on that anything was possible if she tried. Maybe the illusion comes from the ones who don't give us what we search for, and the biggest lessons we learn are from the ones who make us feel like we aren't enough.

Journaling

How can we express our inner voice and convey it in a clear manner on paper? I found myself through writing. Being able to journal allows you to connect with your feelings on a higher level than just in your mind. I had an awakening moment after relaxing in the bath followed by a 30-minute meditation; it opened me up and made me explore emotions that I had never really looked into. I didn't want this to be a "come-and-go moment". By writing down how I felt, I knew I could come back whenever I chose and the words would show so vividly how I felt at that time, recording my growth. As soon as that pen touched to paper, oh my! Words came flushing out that I didn't even know had been locked inside me. Feelings from the past, images of my future – it was all there. So much unveiled itself that my hand was writing faster and faster. I knew this was for all the right reasons.

Two minutes into my journaling I broke down, crying. That deep into my writing, I didn't know exactly word for word what was coming out until I finished my last sentence, as I wanted to get every detail out on paper before it faded from my mind. I gasped and dropped the pen. What had I just experienced? My younger self, who had been locked away, had broken free. She wanted to be a part of the soul again, and all for the better, to bring back that innocent happiness I once had.

I wrapped my arms around myself, a long overdue hug of me. 'I will never lose you again.' You see, we let society and opinions shape us into becoming who everyone else wants us to be. We lose ourselves over these years, but the great news I have to share with you is this: you can go and soul-search and rescue yourself at any time you choose. All it takes is honesty between you, a pen and a piece of paper. You don't have to write yourself an essay; just put what you're feeling down by logging your day. It can be as simple as "not feeling myself today due to arguing with a friend" or "loved today, spending time with my family". The more you journal, the more expressive you will become. That little girl or boy you left when you looked for the approval of others is waiting for you to go and save them! So please, this is a message to find who you are in the silence of your own thoughts, no matter how hard it may be. Don't give up on yourself because you never know when that moment of rescue will come.

Benefits of journaling

1. It relieves stress.

2. Allows yourself to understand your emotions.

3. Sets yourself goals/daily tasks.

4. Organises yourself – creates to-do lists.

5. Jots down random ideas that come to you.

6. Helps you reflect on your day.

7. Improves your mindset.

8. Space to write down your creativity.

9. Helps memory.

10. Helps you let go of anxiety or depression.

It became magic

Maybe you don't believe in magic because you have never experienced it?

What if I told you that once you put your pen to paper that's when you unleash the magic?

Maybe you won't ever have to blow your birthday candles out again to make a wish.

Simply because you trusted the thoughts that were flushed out onto paper, you took action daily to make those ideas happen.

Then one day they became magic.

Exercise: journal your thoughts

What are you holding onto and can't let go of?

....

....

What is missing?

....

....

Write down your goals and visions.

....

....

Who do you want to become? Describe that person.

....

....

....

Manifest

What is manifesting? What does it do? It aligns us with our true purpose after we make decisions about where we want to go and who we want to be. We can't send mixed signals out to the universe or our imagination or we will confuse our pathway. This is why the power of visualisation is key to manifesting. We have to be crystal clear about where we want to go, otherwise we will take the wrong route and it will take us years to get to our destination because we had no clear vision. You wouldn't make a five-hour drive to a new location without putting the correct address on Google Maps, would you? This is how manifesting works. You have to take your mind to exactly where you want to go.

Manifestation is visualising, believing and then taking action. You have to do all three for it to work. You can dream of a holiday all day long – but if you don't put the work in to save for it and have no booking confirmation, then you can't just click your fingers and magically appear in the Maldives. This is how you should look at manifestation. Self-belief – your potential is limitless! But as we get older we lose that confidence along the way. Believing in ourselves and our dreams can cause us to feel so much fear around the thought of living our fantasy life. Deep down, we don't feel deserving enough for it.

We lose our faith along the way, and this is why I want to take it back to basics with you. When you were younger, how magical was it to believe in Santa? You would go to bed imagining him flying across the sky with his reindeer and stopping on top of your roof with his sleigh. He would then shoot down the chimney with all your presents as he gulped all the milk, taking two bites of the mince pies you left him;

and of course, let's not forget, all the carrots were gone! The reindeer loved them! You were either on the naughty or nice list, depending on how you were all year, and the outcome would be that you received presents or coal. How devastated were you when you found out Santa wasn't real? I remember crying every tear out of my body. It felt like a mini heartbreak for such a young girl. I guess it was because believing in magic made life so much more fascinating. The feeling of it being "too good to be true" kept me on my toes. That belief you had in Santa is something you can get back, because that power is created inside. You can bring out that inner child who believed in it all, then you can use that energy to fire it towards your talent and character. Because that spirit is what will take you to your goals, attracting nothing but blessing after blessing with the high energy you vibrate out into this world.

From your previous exercises you have written down your goals and who you want to become. Keep these thoughts close and bring them into the next section for meditating. The next step to making them a reality is by manifesting this into your meditation. You now need to envision how you would feel if you had achieved these goals. Ask yourself: 'Who am I celebrating with?' Then dig deeper: are you crying happy tears? How does that feel? You have to feel it within your whole body and celebrate it as if you have just succeeded! Feel the energy overflow your bloodstreams with achievement and excitement. *Picture it, believe it and then make it happen!* Feel the power and hunger that sit inside you. Grab that ball of energy and never let it go. Show up every day as the person you want to become and watch the beauty that will unfold in front of you. Some will say it's luck, but it will be all down to your dreaming and doing. It's time you stopped tolerating a secondary life. Go and manifest everything your heart desires! This is your opportunity to dig deep into your thoughts.

If you can imagine it, you can create it which means you can make life exactly how you want it to be. Work endlessly on your dreams, and never stop until you make yourself proud – you deserve nothing less. Remember, that child who believed in magic is somewhere deep inside you. Go and tell them what magic you have in store for them today, and maybe you might start believing in Santa again.

If you believe it's yours, my love, then it is.

No obstacles got in the way

One night she went to sleep envisioning her dreams, ready to make them happen.

The next morning, from that day onwards, no obstacles got in the way of the girl's dreams, no matter how tough it was.

Because she already knew

It was hers to have,

If she worked for it.

Meditating

People want to heal but they don't want to make the time for it. They can't face the thought of having to sit with their emotions, because it's too painful. This leads to excuses – pretending they are busy so that they don't have to relive their past events or traumas. If you want change you have to do something; this is why meditating helps. It is such a powerful tool and it's free. It helps you connect more with your soul and has so many other benefits. Below I share some tips on meditating.

Benefits of meditating

1. Brings you back to the present moment.

2. Quietens your overthinking voice.

3. You let go of any anger or pain.

4. Reduces depression/anxiety as it helps you manage stress.

5. Strengthens your creativity/imagination.

6. Teaches you patience.

7. Brings you gratitude.

8. Connects you with your intuition.

9. Changes your perspective/helps you reflect.

10. You make peace with your past.

Don't worry if you find it difficult at first to switch off; it takes time, dedication and practice. Try to find your own little touch on meditating. You might find that being in the bath works better (this is my favourite). Whatever it is, don't give up on meditating. There is no right or wrong way. Keep being consistent, because that is the key to finding yourself – it only works if you do this. So find the way that is best for you.

As you sit there, all your thoughts will go through your body as you start to feel all the emotions you had locked within. They will creep up to the surface of your skin, and chances are you will feel uncomfortable. Remember, this is the beautiful part of meditating – you can get to the root of what's caused you pain, if you give it a chance to release. Your mind will run off into the unknown, bringing more things up, and that's okay – don't panic. Welcome these negative events that have happened; let your emotions flush out of you. Don't be scared to face what hurt you; it's the only way you will heal, when you revisit and let go. When we face the hurt head on, we can call it quits by accepting what caused us pain and getting rid of the dead fruit stored inside, which we left to go mouldy for so many years.

Take yourself off on a journey through your breathing and get ready to see what you lost along the way. You are going to be so free from the day you decide to forgive and accept. This is why meditating is so incredible; this practice teaches you that forgiving others is for your own peace. It helps you manifest the life you want to create as you envision the person you want to become. It helps break you free from what has kept you hidden and strengthens your visualisation as you work towards transforming yourself into the magnificent soul you wish to be. *Make time for your healing. Make time for your growing.*

Now you are ready to meditate, go to a place where you feel calm and can switch off. Go anywhere but your bedroom; let that be the place you sleep. This is your time to create, visualise and get connected with your intuition. Search deeper and feel every emotion. *To heal you have to feel.* Revisit past experiences that you have found painful. Connect with your inner child and accept everything for what has been and that alone will help you cleanse the wounds that need healing. If you don't, you will often respond back to life from that place of pain. It's time to let go, my dear. As you breathe in, ask yourself, 'What is causing me pain?' Then, when you breathe out, place your hand on your stomach, and as you expand let it go – push the negativity right out of your body. All the anger and pain you have carried for so long will no longer serve you when you make that decision to release. Love yourself for all that has been; let your breath take you to the wounds you need to cleanse.

When a random feeling of anxiousness pops up in your day-to-day life, whether you are at work or out with friends, find a place of quietness and take some time out for your breathing. Close your eyes and focus on the sunlight that shines above your head so brightly. Feel the warmth it radiates onto you. Focus on that, then use the same breathing techniques, and every time your mind wanders return it back to that beautiful golden sunlight. When you want to manifest something into your life, close your eyes and create space for all the magnificent ideas you have inside that talented brain. Breathe in, visualise your highest self (I envisioned my book), then, as you breathe out, believe it is yours. Keep repeating, until you believe with every single ounce of you that this vision is already yours.

Tips for meditating

1. Light some candles; set the tone.

2. Play some calming music.

3. Burn sage to cleanse your surroundings.

4. Close your eyes, place your hand on your heart, feel each pump, be grateful for it.

5. Breathe in for a count of 4.

6. Hold for 4.

7. Breathe out for 4.

8. Keep repeating, and after 5 times you will become more relaxed.

9. When your mind starts to wander, that's okay. Return it back to your breath or the calming music you play in the background.

10. Keep it up – you're doing a great job.

Remember, keep practising; don't be so hard on yourself. As we discussed, not every meditation will give you the same experience, but each one is just as important. You are growing, my dear, and that is something to smile about.

We should appreciate our breath. It is the only thing we truly have. Without it, we wouldn't be alive.

Happiness is being in the present

If I asked you now what makes you happy, what would your answer be? Would it be your car? Your £900 shoes? Whatever popped into your mind, keep hold of that thought. I want to take you deeper into what real happiness is.

How many times have we said these words to ourselves? 'I'll be happy when I receive my paycheck' or 'I'll be happy when I meet someone.' When I was younger, I used to think that when I got my own car that would "complete me" and then I would be happy forever because I would have freedom to go anywhere I wanted! Oh boy, how wrong I was.

We have all come across these thoughts before, haven't we? Let's say you are feeling grumpy, hating the world because your nails and lashes aren't done, so that means you can't be happy today! I mean, I understand the frustration to a certain degree, but do you realise what you are putting yourself through? A day of hell, that's what I would say. Unable to crack a smile on your face because you are too anxious to leave the house in case somebody sees your hideous nails. Every time you look at them they are chipped, bringing you a feeling of loathing and disgust to your stomach.

The only way you can be "happy" is to wait until tomorrow comes and your appointment arrives. The day finally comes: you leave the salon feeling on cloud nine! 'A fresh pair of nails, oh yeah!' You think to yourself, 'Could this day get any better?' Then, an hour into your day, an unexpected surprise from a little birdie in the sky comes to say hello. That's it; your whole day is wrecked, all because of that stupid bird!

'This won't bring me any luck – look at the state of my outfit!' Back to square one, and you relive all the feelings you felt yesterday. You see, placing your bet on believing your nails would bring you joy is actually the opposite of "real happiness". It is called short-term happiness, and as soon as that feeling of buzz starts to fade you go back round in circles, stuck in a rut.

How to break the cycle? This is where meditation comes into play. It has a huge impact on our mood; it shines a happiness within. We stop and embrace what is around us. Our bodies get a chance to slow down and appreciate what's around us; that's what real happiness is – knowing that *the best things in life are free*. When the pandemic hit, everyone felt a deep concern for missing out on social connections; their lack of freedom to go out and see loved ones made their souls grieve. We all adapted very well, understanding that our hair and nails would be poor for a few months. But the real pain came from missing out on connections; that is what hurt people most. This is because real happiness is being in the present moment. It is the hugs we give, the sunsets we see and the friends we belly-laugh with, because…real happiness is all about the feeling you have inside. That's why we have to fall in love with how we see life by practising our gratitude list. When you realise this, you will find an internal happiness that will never leave your side for the rest of your life. Because now you know that happiness has never been far away…it is within you.

Soul-search and find that joy, my love.
It's waiting for your arrival.

Find it

Find happiness in all that you do,

In the words you speak,

The souls you help,

The connections you make,

The smiles you brighten.

Make the best out of what you have,

Then you will find happiness in all that you do.

Gratitude

Why is it important to remind ourselves what we are grateful for? Why do we need gratitude in our day-to-day lives? The answer, we find, is: because it brings us happiness within. Be grateful for the hands you shake with, cook with and write with. Be grateful for the eyes with which you capture the beauty within people, and the places you get to explore. Be grateful for the heart that keeps pumping and keeps you loving. Be grateful for the lungs that breathe in the fresh air, be grateful for your legs that you use on your walks. Be grateful for being, living and loving. You owe it to yourself to enjoy your days, not just half-heartedly – full-heartedly is the only way. When you focus on your gratitude list, then guess what? You notice something else to be grateful for, and the snowball effect happens. Count your blessings, not your troubles. The mind is our little bubble and creation. The great news is that we can decide how to decorate. So let your mind take you off to the sunset in your dreams as you wash away those nightmares. Fill it with smiles, sunshine, clouds and glitter, love and joy. Create a more freeing, happier, beautiful today by reminding yourself of what flows around and within you.

Exercise: Your gratitude list

1. ....

2. ....

3. ....

4. ....

5. ....

6. ....

7. ....

8. ....

9. ....

10. ....

Whenever your mood next deteriorates, come back to this chapter and look over your gratitude notes. When you start reminding yourself of who and what you are grateful for, it will make you feel warm and cosy inside, because that's the effect gratitude has on you: it grounds you and makes you feel humble within. Getting into the swing of it takes time, but once you get into a routine with it you never look back, because you know life is all about the little moments, and our job is to remind ourselves of that every single day.

Appreciating

Life is about appreciating the little things.

When you are grateful for what you have,

You'll have everything you will ever need.

The little things

It's all about the little things, like opening up your blinds and making room for the sun to beam through on your lazy Sunday morning. It's the excitement you get on your days off when you curl up in bed with your hot cup of tea as you get cosy under your duvet. The enjoyment you get from filling your bathtub with lots of bubbles. It's lighting a new candle, or writing your thoughts down on paper to settle yourself to sleep. It's the feeling you get when you snuggle up with your blanket every time you watch TV. It's the smell of a new book, and the breeze that travels through your home on a hot summer's day. It's repeating your favourite song over and over again because it makes you feel alive every...single...time. It's doing the things you love constantly because they bring you comfort. It's growing to understand that life is trying to tell us something every time we experience these points in time. It is whispering in our ears daily, saying: 'The little things will fulfil your soul – if you let them.'

So look for them, my darling. They are all around you.
It really is the little things that matter most.

'And what a beautiful reminder it is when you realise how magical the smallest of moments can be.'

@rewiringthoughts_

My pain is not greater than your pain

'Hurting others won't heal your pain inside.'

@rewiringthoughts_

Life really does spin our whole world upside down when we lose a loved one. The pain that sits with us is like a dark cloud sitting over our shoulders. Floating through our days not being able to smile, hardly able to speak, interacting with others is difficult to say the least. When we lose others, we lose a part of us. Goodbyes are the start of grieving, questioning all the whys about life, but our pain is not to be compared. We should support and encourage others to keep going through their journey of pain. Let somebody know there is a light at the end of the tunnel and they will arrive when the time is right. The process is ugly, but it is a part of healing, and supporting each other is the only way we heal ourselves. We are all in it together.

I have a twin sister named Amy. When we were younger you can imagine the arguments we had over who slept in the top bunk bed. She always beat me to it. I was desperate for my own space and room, so when we would go over and sleep at our nan (Dolly) and grandad's (Charlie) house I came up with a plan. I would pack my clothes in a bag and leave them in the spare room every Sunday before my mum and dad came round to pick us up. In the end my plan of attack worked – I moved in with my nan and grandad. I had my own room to myself without having to fight for it. Living with my grandparents started when I was 11. It definitely made me feel like my soul was connected to their generation. Spending most of my weekends with my nan and grandad shaped me into who I was becoming – a wise young lady. Hanging around my grandparents rubbed off on me. I wasn't your typical 18-year-old who was always out and about attending sleepovers with groups of friends. Being at home with my family was where my heart was.

It was the 21st of January 2016 when my grandad passed and my whole world came crashing down. I was 21. The house phone rang at 12:30am. I shot up to see my nan's face in a panic. We were minutes away from losing my grandad; you could already feel the pain kicking in around us. We arrived at the hospital – my nan, mum, sisters and I. Not long afterwards my auntie, uncle and cousins followed. As the car pulled up outside the hospital, I jumped out of that car quicker than lightning, running up every flight of stairs as fast as I could to make it to the ward on time to see my grandad off. As I arrived, the nurse stopped me. She looked me in the eye and said, 'I am so sorry – he just passed.' That was the day that changed my whole life. I was convinced I would have got there on time to see him go, to hold his hand and to kiss him off to see the angels.

Losing my grandad was the first loss I had ever experienced. The pain, the aches, the soul-destroying reality of his presence not being in the house shattered my heart into pieces. Even his smell was everywhere in the house. How could I return to work when a huge chunk of me had gone with him? I wrote a speech for my best friend at his funeral; it honestly was one of the most defining moments of my life. I spoke in front of hundreds of people, sharing my love and stories of our relationship and reminding everyone about his funny humour and amazing ways. As I got to the end of my speech, my throat choked up. I knew this was my last chance to say goodbye.

The lump in the back of my throat didn't shift. The eyes started to fill, and then something magical happened. As I looked up, I saw my nan looking at me, hanging on my last words. Next to her my mum was gripping my nan's hand while she looked at me with pride, seeing her daughter stand and speak. Gazing at my grandad's coffin, I knew I had to hold myself together and say their goodbyes for them and for the rest of our family and members who were in that church that day. As I finished the speech, all I could hear was the applause around the church. It made each and every single hair on my body stand up. I knew I had done my grandad proud. The healing process was painful. I felt numb throughout. The only words that kept going through my mind were: 'If only I could see your face one last time, Grandad.' Those words stuck with me. Crying myself to sleep with them every night – that became my reality.

Returning to work a few days later was hell! I floated through my days on autopilot, not feeling like anybody understood my pain, especially after getting told these very words by my boss: 'You are being moved to the front of the store today. I need you to have your happy face on and stand here and welcome every single customer.' My reply was, 'I have just lost my grandad. I don't feel myself. Can I please stick to my normal job?' The reply kicked me in the stomach. 'I have lost people too, and look, I am still here, so get on with it, kid.' Those were the words that pushed me off the edge. Talk about kicking a dog while it's down! She treated my pain like it was nothing. Was it because she had lost more family members? Or was it because she was having a bad day? and she took out her frustration on me. Whatever it was, she poured her anger onto my pain. She hurt me because she was still suffering. At the time I didn't understand why my boss was so mean to me that day; now I understand. She had so much pain buried inside that every time something sparked her memory it brought back all her pain.

Grieving is a feeling we have to experience. We can't push it aside. We can't bury it within. We have to face it dead on, feeling every heartbreak. If not, we only go around cutting people who didn't even cut us. No matter what pain you have experienced, no matter how little you think other people's situations are, hurting others won't heal you. It will only make the other person suffer more. We have to accept that we all will feel differently, no matter how big or small the situation is.

That day made me realise the impact we have on others – how our words can take us to the darkest places of our minds, standing on the edge of the cliff debating whether or not to jump. Words cut deeply. We don't look closely enough at actions. We listen to words as they make us believe every single sentence, as if our lives depended on them. We are all damaged to the core from losing someone we love. Pain is all around us and we all suffer with some type of pain. We don't have to make pain a competition. It is not a beauty contest, and there shouldn't be any comparison of pain. Instead, you should be filled with compassion for another person's pain, because you have been there and you know that pain sucks. You don't have to experience it to understand another person's pain, but at least respect their feelings and support them.

Make that person's day of pain feel like a moment of healing with your kindness. The best way to heal yourself is to heal another person by listening with love. It will take away somebody's darkness. One scar at a time, faded but never forgotten. My pain is NOT greater than your pain. We are all equal.

Filling your heart up with memories

The people you have lost along the way didn't make you bitter. You knew that being angry with the world for taking away your loved one would not set you free. It's the search deep inside that is the only way for you to move on and forgive. Things didn't turn out exactly how you wanted them to, but the feeling in your heart understands that those lost are being taken care of in heaven. There is no time to hate others just because inside feels broken.

The pain will never wash away, and that's okay. Stories of losing a loved one will help another person who needs it. Life is about reaching out and helping the ones who don't know how to help themselves. If we hurt others because of the pain we feel inside, we know it will only add more burns and discomfort to our life. The broken heart will never go back to how it was before it lost, but it knows it has to accept the loss with grace by holding onto the special memories.

Be grateful for the time you spent together – the laughs, the tears and even the arguments. The day you broke free was the day you decided: no resentment was held in the heart. The growth to understanding that the healing process was under your control, and how you could move forward with life again without them, is up to you. Fill up your heart with the magical memories created in that chapter of your life with them. It's not goodbye forever. The souls always reunite together, one day soon.

We will meet again, my angel.

Grieving

You have every right to feel how you do.

Your heart has shattered into a million pieces and now is the time for you to process this change.

There is no right or wrong way when dealing with your emotions, but I can assure you that

One day you will get to a place where you can look back and laugh about the memories without falling apart.

When they went, a chunk of you disappeared too, and that's okay.

One day at a time, beautiful.

You will get there; slow and steady wins the race.

'There is not a better feeling than making somebody else smile.'

@rewiringthoughts_

You can't fix people

'Everyone's problems aren't yours to solve. People will change of their own accord.'

@rewiringthoughts_

My purpose, I thought, was to fix people, to come up with a solution, to re-enact a scenario so that the person's problem was fixed there and then. I realised that you can only do so much, then the rest is up to them – they have to want to change. Every time my friends and I met up I was their personal coach, which was absolutely fine with me! I loved to help in any way possible, especially when seeing people's energy uplifted by my guidance and support. Every time I helped others, I helped myself. It became a strong passion for me, and this was the turning point that slowly started to shape me into who I am.

I had one friend who needed me there 24/7, which made me get to a point where I was becoming their therapist. Every day I was there putting in 110 per cent cooperation, determined to get her through to the other side. It was like a full-time job in itself for me. My tongue would get tired and my brain would go foggy every time she collapsed mentally – I went down with her.

One day we were both having a coffee. I could vibe that my friend was back to square one with her thought process. I felt a heavy heart inside for her and in that split second of feeling ineffective I didn't know what to say to my friend. I was worn out just as much as she was. All the energy and time I had given over the past few years had added up, leaving me feeling run down, like a car on an empty tank. Every day she would repeat the same topic. Mentally and physically there wasn't any strength in me to find a solution for her this time. I felt I had already said so much. This time, instead, I listened. My usual lectures got put on hold for the entire conversation. Not because I didn't want to give advice, but because there was no energy for me to translate into words.

I would repeat what she said out loud, just to confirm to her that I was there and listening. As we finished our coffee, she gave me a big hug and said, 'Thank you so much for everything. I feel so much better. I would be lost without you.' These words triggered a thought in my brain, which was: 'If my friend feels uplifted from this conversation (which was mostly her venting), then it proves that listening to others is the key to healing.' My awareness felt sharper than a knife. I sat there questioning the power of healing as I digested my friend's words of praise. I had, in fact, done nothing. It was all her. I only asked questions for her to dig deeper so that she could find the answers.

It clicked with me that you can't fix people but you can help them get to the other side. The answer was that my friend was not ready to take any advice I had given her months or years back. She needed to get over the hurdle of how to fix herself when she was ready. We all have moments when we feel we have to come up with a solution for others, otherwise we feel like we have failed them. I have learned from this that the best advice we can give is to listen. When we ask questions of people it strengthens their awareness of how they actually feel, bringing them closer to an authentic answer. Ask: 'What is causing you to feel like this?' This will spark the process of self-reflection, guiding those who are confused to figure out the root to their worries. *Questions spark answers.* This can then make others dig deeper when they are ready to go within more and examine themselves.

Dishing out advice when the person hasn't asked for it is like throwing yourself into the sea without a life jacket. Let's face it, you would drown if you couldn't swim, right? You will only suffocate yourself by trying to drum solutions into other people's heads, especially when that person is not equipped to listen. The power of listening helps others find themselves, hammering away at their own consciousness as they hear their own voice vent out while you sit, question (with sympathy) and listen. They will be grateful to you for being that port of call there at the other end; and that, to me, is the power of advice.

A helping hand

If you are down, I give you my heart.

When there's nobody to listen, I give you my ears.

If you need a shoulder to cry on, I will give you a helping hand...

Then, the moment they get to the other side, they will never forget your kindness, which saved them.

That is the beauty of reaching out:

It always comes back when you need it.

Be kind to others

It breaks my heart to think that so many people have committed suicide due to many different reasons. Please be kind. We all have problems – there are just different types of problems. There is depression, anxiety, paranoia, addiction, disorders, PTSD and plenty more. No matter how well you think you know somebody or their life the reality is you don't. The happiest people can be battling depression. The ones who are always out and about with friends can feel so lonely. People suffer and a smile can hide all of these. So, let's support everyone's mental health by spreading our kindness and respecting their feelings.

People want to feel like they are being listened to; understanding gives us comfort. Think about a time when you just wanted to get stuff off your chest. Did you want the other person to keep talking and come up with an outcome? Or did you just want them to listen and say, 'I am here for you – what can I do to help?' Keeping our ears and heart open for those who need it makes such a difference. For example, somebody with PTSD will have images of their past traumas locked inside their heads, and they can't let go of them. They can't understand why it happened to them and they need answers. They are stuck and don't know how to move forward with life. People with depression or anxiety feel like they are weak because they suffer at times. People with addiction will have moments when they feel hopeless because they can't put a stop to whatever it is they are addicted to. People with disorders don't think they are good enough as they are. The list is endless, and we have to support every single person, because you never know what people are battling behind closed doors.

There are so many people who feel ashamed to openly ask for help, so let's normalise reaching out. Let's normalise seeing it as a sign of strength to admit how you feel – it shows bravery. Let's normalise that we all have our down days. Let's appreciate and support every single person we meet, because as I have got older I have realised this: we are all going through something – it's just different for everyone. If a friend is down, don't assume it's about you. Instead, pull them aside and see what support you can give. Checking in on them will make their whole day. Do not judge the happy faces you see on Instagram or in real life; mostly importantly, don't judge at all as people are so good at hiding their feelings.

If you don't understand how somebody feels then please take their feelings seriously, especially if they share how suicidal they are. It takes a lot for a person to openly state it. If we treat every person we meet with kindness, then the power of saving them can become a reality. If you see something good in someone, tell them. You never know who needs to hear it.

Through my eyes

If you could see yourself through my eyes, you would never speak unkindly to yourself. You would never pull out every flaw or imperfection. You wouldn't ever wish to be somebody else dreaming of living a life that wasn't your own. If only you could see yourself through my eyes, my darling, you wouldn't ever want to change.

You are beautiful just the way you are.

You matter

You matter, even though you can't see it.

You matter, even though you never think it.

You matter, even though you wish to be somebody else.

You matter, because the above doesn't matter any more,

As right now is the day you start appreciating who you are.

Celebrate yourself today, tomorrow and every damn day after that.

'Your kind words could have saved somebody who wanted to say goodbye to the world – be kind always.'

@rewiringthoughts_

Wishing our life away

'Wishing today away by worrying about tomorrow, when tomorrow hasn't arrived and isn't promised.'

@rewiringthoughts_

If Mystic Meg knocked on your door, sat you down and said you had this many years to live, or months, how would you feel? What would you do? I know every time I think deeply about this it makes me more hungry to strive towards my goals. 'Live each day as if it was your last.' That quote sticks in my head – the words we have been reminded of for so many years. It creeps up on social media. It rolls off the tips of our tongues. The question is: do we understand what that quote is trying to teach us?

It is saying you have to live your life for you, doing everything on your terms, exactly how you want it. You have to make a bucket list, travel and explore the places you have always wanted to go. Eat the glorious food and drink the wine (in moderation). Wake up every day and be ready to live it to your fullest potential even on the days you don't feel up to it, still smiling through your down days. Don't wish away your weekdays by hoping for the weekend, as that day may never arrive for some of us – that is the painful truth.

When I was younger my mum and dad were very close with the family who lived opposite us. My twin sister and I would always play outside with the two boys. There was no doubt about it, we girls were tomboys. We would be playing football with them till lunchtime, water fights till teatime. We grew up becoming very close family friends. We would celebrate every birthday party together, growing up through childhood together and sharing the most wonderful memories. When I moved into my nan and grandad's home, high school days were ready to commence. The playing days were over. It was all about entering our next chapter of our lives. As time went on, we all grew apart, and playing outside wasn't as much fun as it had been when we were younger.

The years went by. I turned 17 and running became a hobby of mine. One day I jogged round to my mum and dad's house, and as I got there my mum's face was white. She sat me down and told me the lad across the road, our childhood friend, had passed away; he'd had cancer. My legs were wobbling. As I sat back into the chair my heart was in my mouth, trying to process the news. Just like that, in a blink of an eye, he was gone. He was ten months older than my twin sister and I. His 18th birthday was approaching and he didn't live to see that day. It makes you question life: why? Why him? News that makes you feel like you got lucky and they didn't. That they didn't get the golden ticket out of the Willy Wonka bar and you did. It sucks.

From that day, I kept him with me in my heart. He was there in my head on the days I wanted to give up, knowing he would do anything to be here going through the challenges I am facing. He would be an adult now like me if he were still here. I picture life so differently for him, starting a family, maybe moving abroad, living life exactly how he wanted; but he couldn't. It is ingrained in me that life cannot be taken for granted, not even on my worst days. This is why we have to wake up knowing we are blessed for another day. Being able to breathe has so much meaning behind it; as you wake up, somebody is taking their last breath. As a newborn enters the world, another will leave. It is the uncomfortable truth, the truth that has to be engraved into our brains so that we remember how blessed we are to be on this planet for another day. Don't wish your life away by treating it as if you have another shot, because you don't. You don't want to get to the last few moments of your life and leave the world with regret, knowing you could have done more, been more and created more. So take those risks, no matter how big they feel. It will either happen for you or it won't. If it doesn't work out then it wasn't meant to be; if it does then it was always yours to have.

A clean slate

There comes an age in life where you don't give a shit. You forget about what has been holding you back and you are ready to wipe the slate clean. You know time is ticking and life is waiting for you to enjoy it. That is the exciting part about starting all over again. You take nothing for granted, no messing around... And this time, you love life that little bit harder.

There is a light at the end of the tunnel

If you are on a path in life where you feel like you want to give up, then let me remind you: the world needs your beautiful soul in it. You may feel that the road you are on is very rocky; you may be unsure of who you are and what's coming next. I promise this pain won't last forever. Life is not against you, it is working for you. This journey is not perfect, and you shouldn't wish for it to be.

You may be stuck in a sea of pain, feeling that nobody understands the depths you have travelled to the darkest places. You have cried a tremendous amount and you are tired of being exhausted. The pain you carry is so heavy and you don't know what else to do. You can't see your own value to this world and this is why you think that to not be here is the only way out. Well, it is not, my dear. People need you, and most importantly that little girl or little boy inside you needs you much more. Don't give up on life – it is short anyway. You will have your days of wanting to give up, but the most beautiful thing is that you can always start all over again tomorrow. No matter how many times you fall, the beauty lies within the courageous heart that wants to keep on fighting. That is who you are: a strong, passionate, radiant sunflower ready to grow into its true self. Once you decide to keep going you will see yourself through a new lens, gleaming more brightly than ever before, and when you do, you will realise that your soul was way too precious to leave behind and your smile is too beautiful to never see again. As you grow through this new life, you discover a new love for tomatoes, or you find that all along you had a hidden talent for art. As you face struggles this time round, you hold onto yourself a little tighter, saying: 'Everything is going to be just fine. I am right here with you.' You are okay with the challenges and uncertainty of life, because you know life will always work out in the end and what is coming is greater than what was lost. You fall in love with yourself again. You travel more and see the blue skies that have never looked bluer and the birds that tweet louder, and you see life for the blessing it is. Then you grow to learn that you are your own best friend and that your own opinion of your life is more important than anyone else's. Life this time round is all about giving your energy and love to the people who need it most – you once knew how that felt.

Finally you make it to 90. As you sit back in your chair, you smile so brightly that even the clouds can feel your energy. As you reflect back on your life you see that it wasn't easy but, oh boy, it was a fun ride! If you could go back and do it again, you would in a heartbeat. You are thankful for giving yourself the chance to live on that day you wanted to give in. It becomes clear that life is temporary, just like us all, and no life is ever worth losing.

As you look outside your window you see a little girl; she looks sad. This flashback brings back some memories. You go outside and sit beside her. As you wrap your arms around her, you say: 'Let me share with you a secret. You are exactly where you are meant to be, little one. Life is working for you, not at you. There will be ups and downs, but I promise, if you love life it will love you back a million times harder. Enjoy all the parts of what life has to offer. Take the highs with the lows, and remember you are so needed in this world. You are a warrior, and that power inside you will always pull you to the light. You were born for a reason.' The little girl hugs you so tightly, and as you hold onto her she whispers in your ear, 'Thank you for saving me,' and that is the moment it all makes sense. You had to save yourself so you could save others.

'If you're reading this and you're in a bad place mentally, remember: don't give up in darkness. You will meet the light at the end of the tunnel.'

@rewiringthoughts_

Recreating

A miraculous turnaround happened once the girl knew she was the only one who could get herself back up, rebuilding in times of distress. Once complete, she ran back to life, excited to show this new version to the world. That's the beauty of recreating: you always come back to life different to how you last left it.

Comparison will eat you up and spit you out

'Keep working on yourself – that glow suits you.'

@rewiringthoughts_

I used to think being different wasn't cool. Having nothing in common with everyone else made me feel alone, like an outsider. I mean, I was, but there's nothing wrong with that, apart from society's perception which led me to believe it. I struggled to fit in with groups as there was nobody I trusted enough to turn to. With no connections built, and becoming unsure of who I was, because I had no similarities with others, it crossed my mind plenty of times: 'Why can't I fit in with everyone else when I try so hard?' There is your answer: I was trying too hard. Why is it we spend so much time reading somebody else's script when we have our own lines to rehearse? We let comparison eat us up and spit us out, becoming like everyone else fighting to fit in with the rest of society.

I suffered terribly with acne from a young age, affecting my confidence. When signing into social media, platforms such as Instagram would be the worst because there were so many models with edited photos of their smoothed-out skin, which made me unhappy with the way I looked. It wasn't that I had a problem with those people, but instead that I despised myself for not trying hard enough to be on that level. The fact was, however, neither did they, because these were edited photos, just like mine. 'Why do I have skin like this and everyone else's is perfect?' Whenever my skin had a breakout I became even more obsessed with editing my photos, covering every spot or blemish I could find that appeared on my face. I pushed myself further and further away from the real me and spent time glaring at my phone screen, editing my face so I could be in that Instagram category of "perfection".

It is so easy to become tangled in the obsession of achieving ultimate beauty when there are tools that encourage you to look like this. They can even go as far as rearranging your facial structure, which is absurd. There is no such excellence, and even if you feel you have made the perfect portrait, soon the urge to post again will come back around, doubling the pressure of editing to the same standard. It is something we should never aim to be. We think editing our photos is the only way we will get approval from anyone in this day and age. I know that because that's what I used to believe – thinking the grass is greener. I have learned the hard way that it's not.

It all stems from our teenage days, when we become most vulnerable and pay attention to the words of others. When growing up and getting comments thrown at me every now and then for having freckles and big lips, it made me wish to be like somebody else. Every day I covered up my freckles before school because the feeling of being different made me feel ugly. Now people draw freckles on their face with make-up and have lip enhancements to get fuller lips. Society's opinion of beauty is forever changing, and we shouldn't try to fit in with our environment, otherwise we will lose ourselves every single time. These bubbles are floating everywhere and it's so easy to become attached.

There is no description or checklist as to what beauty is, and to think I didn't feel it enough, because I wasn't like everyone else, was so pessimistic of me. When I accepted that I would never be like them, or like the edited person from my photos, that was the day I began to love myself for all that I am. I deleted my editing app and instantly felt like a huge weight had lifted off my chest. All I could do after that was sit and appreciate the courage it had taken to remove myself from that deadly confined space. It is a showcase for the people that you barely know, craving likes from those we haven't met and being popular with people who don't truly know us. It's crazy to think this generation bases our values through the likes we get. We really don't need editing apps. They will never change anything in the world. They are just a quick fix that is really making us lose our confidence with who we are. There is nothing that shines brighter than a soul who doesn't pretend to be anyone else but themselves.

Start today by paying attention to the things you consume. Detox from your social media. Unfollow anyone who makes you question who you are. Make Instagram a place to learn, not compare. Every time you scroll, think of the amount of time you are wasting when you could be dedicating it to growing into the person you are destined to be. Cleanse yourself, and follow pages such as motivational speakers, healthy cooking guides and travel inspiration. Whatever floats your boat for positive reasons, do more of that! They say you are what you eat; it is the same for what you watch, read and listen to – you slowly become it. Make sure that what you consume is positive, and remember: don't try so hard to become somebody you're not – you will only disconnect you from you.

Next time you don't feel good enough, that is the moment when you need to dive in and act by reminding yourself that being different is cool! Write in your journal: 'I am my own beautiful, and I am so proud to look and be who I am. I will never stop reminding myself of this.' So stop comparing yourself to others, stop wishing for somebody else's life. Stop feeding yourself with negative self-talk and start focusing on improving yourself. Become the greatest YOU you can be. There will never be another you, and that alone should give you the courage you need to start all over again.

Just as you are

Maybe comparison came from that heartbreak? Feeling like you weren't enough, but it had to happen so you could realise how much better you are without them. He didn't cheat on you because you "weren't enough", he just didn't see the value of your type of love; and hey, who wants to be with somebody who cheats anyway? What life would that bring you? A life of paranoia, and you don't deserve that. You wish for a meaningful relationship, and what you seek is still going to happen. Wait – the right one is coming. Don't compare yourself to the girl he cheated with behind your back. Don't waste one more tear on somebody who doesn't have your best interests at heart. Because the older you get, the more you realise that the only people you want to be surrounded by are the ones who do appreciate you. You may be thinking: how do I shake off the aches and pains? The answer is to keep moving. Don't stay stuck in the same place of heartbreaks – let this teach you to love yourself more. Please listen to me when I say you are better off without them. One day you will look back at this moment and be so glad you carried on walking. Give yourself a chance, my darling, and leave behind the people who mistreat you. They're not worth it, but guess what? You are!

Just as you are is already enough, and it will be more than enough for the right person.

Comparing your life to others'

We have all been there, putting ourselves down. You think your life or business isn't enough because you compare it with somebody else's. But little do you know that the person you're trying to match with could have been working all their life just to get where they are now. Success doesn't happen overnight; it is a process. You shouldn't compare your first chapter to somebody's 100th chapter – it's different for us all.

Comparison is everywhere and it amazes me how much we humans compare ourselves to everything and everyone. When starting my quote page '@rewiringthoughts_' I had so much confidence in my work that it never made me compare. If anything, it made me want to support other business pages every time I saw them come up on my timeline. I knew they could never do my page like me and I could never do their page like them, and that's it. So many people spend their time looking at other people's social media pages more than their own; this is where self-doubt kicks in. If you look at other people's work and find it hard to be inspired, then that answers your question as to why you get down.

The key to overcoming comparison is blocking out what other people are doing. Watching their every move won't get you to your destination more quickly. This is why people are often sidetracked, because they think if another business is doing great then they have to do the exact same. I have learned that you don't need to do what everyone else is doing in order to succeed. Put your own stamp on your tasks and make it your own. We spoke about having all the answers inside, and you, my friend, have them in there. Focus on your own content and forget about what others are doing, then you will get to where you need to be. Chances are you are doing better than you thought, and comparing yourself to everyone else only shines the light away from your own success. Comparison will kill your talent. If you struggle to feel motivated about your business then I suggest you mute people's pages, but only the ones who make you second-guess your potential. It works – try it.

When your self-esteem is low, it is pretty hard to convince yourself that there are people who look up to your work when you feel it isn't good enough. But I can promise you that there are so many out there who are inspired by you daily, just as you are inspired by them. Take the attention off what others are doing and stay in your own lane by believing in your talent, and guess what happens when you keep being your own cheerleader? You make it! The moment you stop comparing, it will grow that voice within, making you realise that the only person you should compete with is yesterday's version of you.

'People's hatred and jealousy towards you
will never block your blessings. It will only
block their own. Remember that.'

@rewiringthoughts_

Relationships

A large number of relationships are killed because of comparison. Let's say a friend could be driving a really fancy car and that could cause the friendship to fade because of your stinking jealous attitude. Or maybe your friend gets a job and you can't be happy for them because you haven't found one yet. Getting bitter over other people's success will only come back around to bite you on the arse. You can always tell when a person isn't happy for you, sensing their energy, like a dog with a bone. If the people around you are envious then you need to get new friends; your circle should be proud, not jealous.

Relationships crumble because of the insecurity people carry inside them; the reality is that we all have insecurities – it's how we deal with them that triggers us inside. If we ignore our inner feelings, we will offload them onto everyone else, leaving them drained. If others do well, that doesn't mean you won't. It's just that the timing is off. Trust that. People who are celebrating their successes have had to plant the seeds and do all the work you are doing right now. So don't let other people's success make you feel insecure about yourself, otherwise it will kill the relationships with yourself and others.

How many times have we heard, 'She got lucky and I didn't'? It wasn't luck but simply that the timing was right for them. If something hasn't happened or worked out for you yet, then don't quit. I have learned that just because you want something now doesn't mean you are ready for it. You have to keep building on your skills and working towards that breakthrough. Supporting another person's success won't ever take away yours from you. Trying to dim somebody else's light won't make you shine brighter either. There is so much room for everyone to succeed. We are all born to be great, all deserving a piece of the cake. Fill your heart up with pure love, not poison. Remind others how talented they are on their best and worst days. Never stop emphasising the good you see in them. Look at it as "if you win, I win", and that's what life is all about – filling each other's cups up with pure love. Never let your insecurities kill all the greatness you have in relationships with others.

Inner peace

Inner peace is the feeling of contentment with where you are in life. Not trying to control situations; just letting them be. It brings a sense of calmness to who you are and avoids the external distractions of people's opinions about you. Nobody can disturb the peace within because you have already cemented a strong love for the person you are and no evil will have the opportunity to change that.

It takes me back to my younger days when my inner peace got destroyed. There was a social media platform called Piczo. People would copy your profile picture and paste it onto a head-to-head with another person. You would wait anxiously to see who people were voting for as their idea of "pretty". I remember getting put on these head-to-heads almost every week, and nervously refreshing the page, waiting for people to tell me I was beautiful. How sad is that? It makes so much sense to me now that no wonder we grow up comparing ourselves to others – our environment has not shown us anything different. As I think back to those years it makes me feel so concerned for today's generation of young girls, as comparison is growing at a fast pace. I was nine or ten years of age when this battle of the prettiest would commence. Sitting there at my computer wasting my days away, searching for the validation of somebody else to save me – it was so damaging. Letting my inner peace slowly dissipate by choosing to believe the external nonsense that was surrounding it all.

If I could go back in time, I would drag that little girl away from that website and leave people to judge among themselves; that was not my business. However, I made it mine as I chose to read and believe it all. No wonder it took me so long to finally accept myself for who I was and what I looked like. That little girl I once was became obsessed with how I was viewed by others. If you can relate, then make a pact right now to stop giving your attention to negative surroundings. It will only block your potential and bring suffering inside, creating more insecurities that will mount up for another day. So walk away from anything or anyone who loves to feed you with bad energy. Remember to invest your time in the places that will make you flourish. Prioritise your happiness first, stay in your lane and mind your own business. You are worth so much more, and no person or social media is ever worth losing yourself for.

Self-worth

Many people think self-worth is based on how they look or what they own. It is not defined by how much money you have in the bank or what clothes you wear either. It has nothing to do with any of this, yet we still struggle with finding our true potential because we believe these materialistic things bring us happiness or grant approval from others. It is so sad to think we can sit on social media for hours on end comparing our life to somebody else's. We think the grass is greener on the other side, moulding ourselves into the people we compare ourselves with. We pull apart every flaw which we consider ugly because our society regards scars, spots and flared-up skin as unnatural beauty, when, in fact, it is the opposite – it is what makes us who we are. Please stop trying to change. Accept that you are enough.

If you own shoes that cost £8 compared to somebody with a pair that cost £800 then that does not make you less worthy. I hear so many people label others as 'idols' because they have materialistic things. You won't get closer to understanding your own worth by putting others on a pedestal. Trust me, these objects are temporary, just like life is. Things with a price tag don't define you. Buy expensive things and enjoy them, but if you can't afford it then you shouldn't. If you can't afford designer gear then so what? But let me ask you this: would you really spend all your money to buy all these clothes if you weren't going to post them on Instagram? How would you feel about yourself if you didn't have to post online? Would you love your body more? Would you stop trying to impress people you don't know? This gets me thinking so deeply, because I have been there. Before a holiday in 2018 (I will touch on this in the next section), I spent so much money on outfits, with notes saved in my phone from morning to night about accessories, about shoes, even about how I was going to style my hair (yes, I am being serious). I became obsessed with other people's idea of me. I was buying clothes for all the wrong reasons. I knew my Instagram feed was going to be full of holiday pictures. People would be viewing my stories, so I had to look a certain way. Now I don't think about what I'm going to wear or post, because my perspective has changed. In addition, I have saved a lot of money from not buying unnecessary stuff, such as clothes I don't need. Your self-worth has got nothing to do with what you have or haven't got. Let's ask ourselves this: who made up the rules that say 'If you don't wear clothes over £300 you're not cool enough'? It's a load of shit. You could wear anything and pull it off, and I know this as I once wore my nan's blouse for a dance show – it looked great, and guess what? Nobody knew! Apart from my mum and two sisters, who still to this day love to bring it up. In all honesty I am glad I can give them something to look back and laugh about. But the point is that it's not about what you wear, it's about how you wear it. You could wear a bin bag as a dress and glam it up with a belt, jacket and heels, then watch it become a new fashion trend. So please, stop comparing what you haven't got to what other people have got. You can't compare yourself to materialistic objects, and what's inside of you is worth so much more, believe me.

Worship yourself

I have been there, following the lives of so many celebrities on Instagram, watching their stories, knowing more about what they were having for tea than about my own life. Sucked into the rabbit hole of what everyone else was doing made me clone this different lifestyle, so far away from who I actually was. About that holiday: it was summer 2018. I went to Los Angeles. Travelled from there to Las Vegas, then finished the magical trip back in California. It was the most memorable holiday I have ever had, for two reasons. Firstly, I laughed, loved and created the most beautiful experiences. Secondly, my own personal reason, I was lost in the trap of Instagram for all the wrong reasons.

How could I forget this memory? I was trying so hard to become society's Instagram model, as I thought this was how I should look to be accepted. I would have to be by a background that was Instagrammable. I now look back at these photos and I can't help but amaze myself, because I don't recognise who that person was. I was so lost, and I didn't even know it. I shake my head as I write this with disgust of how caught up I was with editing my face; it was unnatural. I mean, I think we wouldn't all be so worked up about a few spots or blackheads if we didn't live in a world where "smoothed-out skin" was a thing. Social media is a fake world but we tend to live in that universe more than our real one, and this is why we become so lost. Technology is huge, photographs can be edited, bodies can be changed and noses can be slimmed down. What for? The approval of others? Do we have to change our bodies and noses for a few likes? You won't find self-worth within the likes of Instagram. We have grown into thinking that acceptance from others is more valuable than what we think of ourselves. We see beauty as being perfect with no imperfections. In fact those imperfections make us stand out, radiating our own beauty.

Now I have come out the other side, I will walk around the supermarkets with my spots on show and, in the nicest possible way, I don't care who thinks what. There was once a time where I couldn't even look at another stranger without thinking 'They are judging my spotty skin' or 'My greasy hair! They will think I am a scruff.' Now I embrace myself for all that I am, even on the greasy hair days! I say this because we all get it! Seriously, nobody cares about us as much as we think they do. The truth is that those Instagram models have greasy hair and a few spots from time to time as well. This is reality! Don't believe everything you see.

My clear head makes me spot somebody I once used to be from a thousand miles away. I can see the red flags next to what I once used to do and this is why I want to touch on this subject, so I can remind people that who you are is always enough. I would change my hair colour for other people – how sad is that? Opinions were thrown at me – 'Go blonder, go darker' – and little Miss Katie would do it. I was forever changing for the approval of others rather than asking myself, 'What do I like best?' I was always putting somebody else's opinion above my own. So next time you do something, I want you to ask yourself: 'Who am I doing this for?' Keep that question with you at all times and remember that people's opinions have absolutely nothing to do with you. Find your own voice. Do what you want, have an opinion, make choices that suit you, and – most of all – be your own spokeswoman!

The only way we will chase our dreams is by discovering who we are. We are all equal souls and nobody came into this world with a gold trophy in their hands. Yet we give special treatment away without any hesitation to those we idolise. I can't express how life-changing it is when you block out what everyone else is doing and start focusing on your own life. People wonder why they aren't getting to where they want to be, and it's simply because they look to see what everyone else is up to. If you go searching for what you view from others, then

I guarantee you will get distracted from your own goals and become sucked into the environment of comparison. You won't find yourself in others. You are the greatest investment, so treat yourself like it! Take those you worship off the pedestal you have held them on for so long, and place yourself back at the top where you belong. Worship yourself and get that crown back, baby!

Your imperfections shine

~~~~~~~~~~~~~~~~~~~~~~~~

That freckle under your eye, that dimple on the side of your
cheek, makes you unique.

You don't need to change anything about you.

Embrace being the magnificent soul that you are;

Grow each day bringing out more and more of what's inside of you.

My darling, your imperfections shine so brightly.

The moment she saw her beauty

~~~~~~~~~

She'd had enough of comparing herself to everyone else, so she took herself on a walk to the park to find a lake, and as she bent down her reflection looked back at her. It was much more beautiful than she had ever imagined, and she didn't understand why she had compared how she looked to everyone else. Her identity gave a big smile back and yelled, 'You don't need to be beautiful like her. You can be beautiful like you!' From that day on, she never compared herself to anyone ever again. And I guess that the most beautiful reminders are the ones that show us our own reflection.

'She grew from having the most beautiful conversations with herself.'

@rewiringthoughts_

You have to keep moving

'What is coming is much greater than what has passed. Believe that.'

@rewiringthoughts_

Maybe you are reading this going through a break-up, or you have just lost your job. Whatever it is, you are stuck in the mud and you need to get yourself out. 'How?' you are thinking. Well, this is why I am here, so let's start!

Life has a funny way of redirecting us and removing us from places that no longer serve us. Trying to take life on the chin is very challenging, especially when you have lost everything. Of course you are going to feel like a failure at life if you have lost that job you were in for five years or the ten-year relationship that was supposed to last a lifetime. It was a huge chunk of you that has now gone, and all that remains is the feeling of lost time. I get it – you are finding it difficult to sum up exactly why this has happened. You sit there questioning, 'Why me?' You get into a habit of this self-doubting cycle because you can't help but wish this wasn't happening to you. This leaves you thinking your life is messed up, but you have to understand that this is happening to get you onto the right path. Don't frustrate yourself wishing things had turned out how your mind projected them to be. Sometimes the things we want most don't deserve us.

Negative self-talk is what is keeping you stuck in the same place. Life will smack you in the face with uncertainty a million times, but you have to remember that the key to breaking free is to keep moving. That doesn't mean it's easy, but if you stay in the same spot you will never get to what's meant for you, and isn't that what you want? To get to a place where you are living freely. This is why it is so important that you trust the change that is taking place in your life. No matter how heartbroken it feels, you keep moving. The choice to move on is yours. It always has been.

Heartbreak

Thank you for breaking my heart.

You made my sight become clear,

Even though it took me a while to finally see it.

If you hadn't broken my heart, I would never be who I am now.

Finally I know that you never deserved me in the first place.

What a beautiful reminder that is.

Embrace the problems

I am 95 per cent certain that most of you will see this subtitle and frown with confusion. Embrace problems? 'What on earth is she talking about, the silly woman? She doesn't even know half of the things I have been through!' The problem is that we expect not to have problems, so that makes us unable to handle them every time they come around. Nobody wants thunderstorms, but they have to come so that sunnier days will soon follow. Life is about accepting what arrives and reminding yourself that the storms don't last forever.

We hold onto the pain, anger and resentment of past events. There are people who are still angry over something that happened ten years ago. If this is you, let me ask: how are you ever going to live a life of abundance if you are still holding onto your past? You either let the problems that have been and gone control you or you control life – you choose. I am not saying it's easy, like a walk in the park, because it's not; but when you choose to move forward with the events life throws at you, then that's when you claim your life back. If life worked out so perfectly for us day in, day out, how boring would that be? Imagine never having to work for anything or go through a few struggles – where would the growth come from? How would we be able to become better versions of ourselves when we have nothing challenging us? Embrace the problems, embrace the uncertainty, as there is something to be learned from each one.

Let go of anything that has broken you. Turn that pain into a journey of growth. Embrace the unknown and let it take you to places you have never been. Let it transform you into a new you by letting it make you instead of break you! Move forward with the pain that mounts up inside you. Let that push and motivate you towards everything your soul desires. Even when you can't see anything changing, it doesn't mean you aren't unlocking new doors – believe that! When something is going wrong it is natural to think our life is heading in the wrong direction, when actually it is the universe taking us to a greater path. We had to be rejected to be redirected. The no's and the heartbreaks all happen for a reason. People leave your life because their time has expired, and in order for you to grow you have to go on without them. Things and people will be lost along the way – the list is endless; but you have to have faith in what is happening, as it is always for a greater reason.

Practice loving a good no, and thank the people who give them to you! Don't fear rejection, don't sit with the heartbreaks – let life kick you in the teeth with it, because that's all it is: a little kick of redirection. Let it go, don't sit and curl up in a ball every day trying to figure out why this is all happening to you. Not everything needs to be figured out, and not everything needs an explanation. Don't expect life to throw amazing blessings at you when you don't make the effort to ride through the storm. You have to move forward with that inner beast inside of you. Get up and show up for yourself every day, then watch the wonderful surprises life has up its sleeve for you. When you receive your next heartbreak, or hear your next no, or break away from a friendship, then you'd better get excited, because life is just about to get started for you. Keep moving!

Fate

I believe what is happening right now is for a reason.

I choose to move forward with fate.

I choose to embrace the change that comes my way. I trust this next chapter, no matter how foggy it is.

Fate will take me to where I need to be next, and I can't wait to see what's on the other side.

Ride with the wind

You aren't supposed to fight back against the wind, you are supposed to flow with the unexpected. Hold tight, trust the wind; it wants to take you somewhere new. Close your eyes and let the breeze sweep you off your feet. Let it take you to the undiscovered. Let it open your eyes to new adventures, showing you why things went wrong while you discover what's right, and hey, you might never want to come back to the place you are fighting to stay in. So let go and enjoy this venture. I have a feeling this new destination that's waiting for you...is already yours to stay.

'You love and you lose. You make mistakes and you get back up again. The beauty lies within the process of us growing as we head to exactly where we are meant to be. Even if we can't see it, we always end up where fate takes us and there is something so magical about that.'

@rewiringthoughts_

Who gives a sh*t?

'Life is too short to hang around toxic people.'

@rewiringthoughts_

Let's cut to the chase here, no messing around. Stop giving a shit about the people who don't care for you. It's as if we let them dangle a carrot in front of our eyes and let them say what they want and we will be hypnotised by it. Being the people pleaser I once was made me take everything to heart – 'She's too much, she's too loud.' The best one was 'Urgh, she doesn't shut up talking.' I mean, they got that one right. I think the process never ends, not even in my sleep.

It would be how they perceived me that would crush me inside. I could have been having the best day, feeling great, then that one comment would get thrown at me and I would let it get into my head. After coming back from my injury, my reply to everything was: 'Who gives a shit?' Somebody doesn't like me? Who gives a shit? They think I'm too much? Who gives a shit?! You have to change your perspective as to what is important enough to care about. Our health? Absolutely! Our opinion of ourselves? Absolutely! The opinions of others? Absolutely not! No wonder people are walking around with the world on their shoulders, because they are letting the opinions of everyone else weigh them down. What people say about you is none of your business. It is only yours if you make it yours.

Free yourself; let go of other people's opinions. What people say about you is a reflection of themselves. Their backlashes are underlining problems that they haven't solved inside. Don't take it personally – laugh it off. Keep your head high. Stop letting people's evil eat you up inside. Walk away from it – you are better than that. You don't have to fight every battle. It's not worth losing your energy for. You win every time you rise above the drama so don't let their spiteful words or made-up lies break you. Let them waste their time, let them believe what they want to believe – the main thing is that you know who you are inside. The people who know you wouldn't second-guess that either.

Your life's purpose is not to be understood by every single person you meet. It is to live by understanding who you are and doing what pleases you! It took me years to figure out that not everyone will understand you and that's okay. Some people will be apprehensive while others will want to get a sense of who you are. Choose the individuals wisely who can have access to you. We all want to live a stress-free life, but not everyone is willing to walk away from the drama to save their peace. People think walking away is a sign of weakness, but it's strength – it shows you don't care what is made up about you; that both your happiness and health is more important than their lies. Realise that opinions are just that – opinions. It's carrying them with us along the way which will damage us. Stop wasting your time fighting for those who won't stick around when you will need them most.

If you are looking for a new motto, let this chapter be it: who gives a shit? Block your ears from hearing what others say and start opening your ears to your own feelings. When you do, you will never lose sight of what really matters. It will become so clear that the shit you used to worry about was so unimportant and, moving forward, the only shit you should ever care about is what you feel inside for yourself. That's what's important.

PS: I think I forgot to mention…

Who gives a sh*t?

Respect yourself

Respect yourself enough to walk away from the ones who try to tell you who you are.

You know who you are better than anyone else.

Never let others bring you down because they can't see the real you.

Don't try to impress the ones who don't respect you.

When they don't see your worth,

Don't take it personally. It only proves how much they shouldn't be in your life.

Your worth is much more than that.

Respect yourself enough to put yourself first.

Go and free yourself, my love.

Let go of the toxic friends

If you are surrounded by people who are negative, then most likely you're going to be negative too. We hold onto so many friendships because we have known others "all our lives", but if the people around you are toxic then you need to get rid of them. Sounds harsh, but when it comes to protecting your inner peace it is always worth it. It doesn't matter how long you go back, even if you both went to nursery together; what matters is your growth and who you are surrounded by. You wouldn't hold onto a pair of jeans with holes in, so why hold onto a friendship that you have outgrown just like those jeans? Some people will get intimidated by your progress, determination and growth, because it makes them feel uncomfortable. Don't stop shining just because your brightness blinds them.

You deserve to be around the people who love and care for you so much. Life is too short to hang around with people who don't lighten up your soul anymore. I have cut many people out of my life when they became toxic, and I don't regret any of my decisions. I knew it was the right thing to do. Who cares what they say? Who cares what they think? You don't have to sit and explain yourself as if you are being judged in court. You have no explanations to give. It's simple – just snip-snip and cut them off. Don't be scared to cut the meanies out of your life! You are better being alone than being surrounded by people who love to bring you down and don't care for you.

Stop trying to save friendships that are already dead. Hanging around with people who don't value or care about you will make you feel depressed. Period. Don't settle for it. You will outgrow a lot of people when you start doing you. We tend to hold on to relationships when we feel a disconnection, but maybe that's the problem that attachment brings. Your real friends or partner will come the moment you decide to let go of the ones who are no good for the soul. Focus on making your circle full of the supporters, motivators and lovers. Life's too short to be around the people who are no good for you.

'I don't want to settle for friendships that don't lighten my heart anymore. I am outgrowing my old self and if that means I have to lose people along the way then I know that's for the best.'

@rewiringthoughts_

Letting go

I won't hold on any longer.

You didn't come back, and I won't force it.

But that's okay, because I now understand that we were never meant to be,

Otherwise you would have been mine.

Don't get bitter, don't get even

There have been so many times when people in my past have not understood or listened to me. So many times when I could easily have bent down to their level and called them mean names in return, or reacted the way they did. Instead, I blocked them. Yes I did – sure did, baby – and it felt great!

I realised I had the power to handle situations. Conflict became easy because I knew my worth, which meant I wasn't scared to stand up for myself. There have been times where I could have got bitter and got even, just to get under the other person's skin, but I knew that the only person I would annoy to the high heavens was myself. It wasn't worth it. Fighting your corner until you are drained to the bone is just not normal. Say how you feel, stand your truth and stick up for yourself, then block them. You don't have to know what the other person's reply is, and it doesn't matter what they think either. There will be so many times people will go out of their way to hurt you on purpose, or maybe it might be a misunderstanding; but either way, if they don't trust or believe your truth then you have to walk away.

You don't have to bow down and kiss anyone's feet just for their approval, and if anyone makes you feel like you have to then, seriously, cut them off. Let them be their own slave in their prison. Don't let them make you become theirs. You can go and find a new best friend who fits in with your needs and hobbies perfectly. There are 7.8 billion people in this world. Don't let one person break you. Walk away elegantly. Don't get even, don't get bitter.

Surround yourself with people who bring you sunshine

Life is about having friends who set your soul on fire. Who you dance on the tables with as you belly-laugh the whole night. They're the type of friends who cheer you on when you are winning, who push you to aim higher. The ones who pull you through your down days by telling you how proud of you they are. The ones who walk beside you through thick and thin and troubled waters, being your life jacket when you need them to be. The ones that answer the phone at three o'clock in the morning, supporting you no matter what. It's the soul sister connection that makes you go through this life together knowing that, wherever you go, you stick up for each other and hold each other's hand all the way through. That, to me, is pure friendship.

You deserve to be around the people you feel safe with. Those who truly care, who never want to see you get hurt – not on their watch! It's about being around the ones who understand you when you go quiet. They don't turn their backs on you. They want to help you. It's the ones who you can act silly with and repeat yourself over and over again and they will never get bored of listening, because they love you.

Search for the quality in friendships, not quantity. If you haven't found that friendship yet then I want you to know that life is full of surprises. You can find your best friend at 30, 40 or maybe 50. It's not about the time, it's about the moment that captures it all. It won't matter at what age you find each other, because once your souls connect it will feel like you have never lived without each other, and that's what friendships are all about – fate bringing you together with people who pop up in your life when you least expect it and prove how much they want to stay. Life changes all the time. The people you thought you would stay friends with, you outgrow; the relationships you thought would last a lifetime end. But the beauty is…it all happens for a reason: to benefit you. There is something so comforting about that.

Keeping them close

It's about the relationships that spin your world upside down
for all the right reasons,

Changing that stormy day into a day of sunshine.

The ones that get you over the rainbow, finding that pot of gold.

They are the friendships that you need to keep close,

Locking them inside your chest.

'I'm not going to complicate it – get rid of the people who are bringing you down.'

@rewiringthoughts_

Don't hold onto your negative thoughts

'Don't run away from your feelings. Sit with them, let them be and let them go.'

@rewiringthoughts_

I used to feel guilty for having days where I wasn't my happy cheery self. Especially as I was a positive person, I used to think: 'How can I be positive if some days I feel negative?' I have learned that it's okay to feel hopeless sometimes. Locking yourself in a cage mentality won't help. You are human; you are allowed to have your down days just as much as you are allowed to have your ups – your feelings are valid. The key to dealing with your negative emotions is to give them a name. My method is by calling mine 'negative Nancy', and every time she comes back around I say: 'Oh, here she is, negative Nancy, here to pop by.' Naming my emotions gave me so much clarity to help me move forward away from them. Saying hello to acknowledge your emotions gives them permission to be there; that way you can accept them more quickly, let go and start recovering your self-love.

Imagine this: you have a balloon flying above your head. That balloon is your emotions. You wrap its string around your arm, which means you have attached the emotion to you. Then you question that balloon and everything about it. All day every day you keep that balloon gripped onto you, and now you feel worse. Now picture this: that same balloon flies over your head and you acknowledge it and welcome it for being there. You don't wrap the string around your arm, because you don't want to make yourself feel any worse than you do. Sooner or later that balloon drifts away, and you realise it doesn't last forever – nor do your emotions. They may be there a whole day or not even for an hour. Either way, they will go as quickly as they came, and it's up to you how you respond to that balloon. Are you going to sit and question it or are you going to accept your feelings and say hello then goodbye? Let it flow through you, let it be and let it go.

It's okay not to be okay

It's okay to hurt. It's okay to cry. Don't bottle everything up just because you feel weak for feeling. Your emotions do not define you, so please stop punishing yourself for having them. Be gentle with yourself. You are going to get through this. Look at everything else you have overcome. Let yourself feel before you can heal because, I promise, this is all temporary. Accept your emotions; don't let them control you. Take a deep breath in and remember who you are. Don't overthink it and never let your mind play tricks on you. You can overcome anything because the strength you hold inside outweighs your emotions. You are human and what comes with us is a whirlwind of emotions and feelings. So, accept yourself on your worst days, because that is when you need the most love. Step up your self-love game and remember to have patience with yourself. Take the time you need in order to recover and don't feel guilty for feeling your emotions. It's okay not to be okay at times. Never forget that.

Please be kind to your precious mind.

Learning to understand your own emotions

The conscious and the subconscious minds are divided into two, and I want to touch on their roles.

Conscious mind: This is your mature side. It's explicit, it's super slow, and we don't control it as much as we would like to.

Subconscious mind: This is your inner child coming out to play. It's implicit, it's fast like lightning, and it's the one we need to take control of instead of letting it take control of us.

Imagine you pour a little bit of juice into a cup and fill the cup with water. Our conscious mind is the juice, which is the small five per cent, then the subconscious mind is the water, which takes up 95 per cent of the glass. Crazy to think, isn't it, that our subconscious mind mostly takes control? We like to think our conscious mind takes charge, that we are the captain of our own ship and that we consciously think with the mature side of our brain. But actually we don't. Have you ever had an argument and said something you didn't mean? It just came out? This is because our subconscious mind is like lightning – it comes out so fast we let things slip out, just like that child who doesn't think before it speaks. It takes a while for the mature side of our brain to catch up, and this is why it is so important to take a step back and ask yourself: 'Is this worth me getting involved?' We begin to see things from a fresh perspective, and when you ask questions like the above you will reprogramme your conscious mind and choose healthier options.

Don't be scared to make mistakes

Our subconscious mind loves to bring up our past and repeat the mistakes we have made, so it's no wonder overthinking happens a lot. You have to not take your thoughts too seriously. You are allowed to make mistakes, and the reason people get down is because they think they shouldn't be making them. You are not supposed to walk through life being perfect. Perfection doesn't exist. Mistakes shape us into the person we are destined to be, making us grow and shine more brightly than ever before.

So many people give up because they didn't overcome the first hurdle they came to. They let the self-doubt kick in, and they say, 'I failed because I wasn't good enough.' Let's say you turned that around and you accepted your mistakes for what they were, saying to yourself, 'I can see why that didn't work – I will keep trying until I will make it.' Don't be scared to pick yourself back up. That's what life is about – finding the courage to stand up tall again, no matter how many times it didn't work. Be ready to make mistakes, stand tall with your Hoover and clean up your own mess! The dirt you clean will make you see more clearly what you need to do next. The journey is beautiful, and we tend to say about our mistakes, 'This isn't for me', when actually the hiccups we make are life lessons, transforming us into our higher self as we become a greater version than who we were yesterday; and that, to me, is pure magic.

You are a masterpiece, and this is just one part of the puzzle. The seeds are being planted by the actions you take daily, depending on what you do. You either sit and dwell on your mistakes or you get back up and try a new way. Which one is it going to be? I think I already know the answer. Mistakes are a part of the process. Nobody said it was easy, but I can promise you it's worth it. If you don't make time for it, don't expect it to happen. Get ready for the magic, because hard work pays off!

And when you want to give up, remember why you started.

'Stop being so hard on yourself. You will mess up and make mistakes but appreciate you can always pick yourself back up. There is so much growth that comes from learning.'

@rewiringthoughts_

Be kinder to yourself

It is not a choice to have depression. It comes out of nowhere and sucks out all the energy you have inside until you feel numb and disconnected from everything around you. If you are suffering right now, I want to let you know that you will get through this, my dear. You are stronger than you think, I promise.

There will be days when you want to switch off from the world and hide. Give yourself permission to have a day off to sulk and feel how you do, but remember: try not to stay stuck in that place for too long. The little voice inside your head will tell you anything to keep you stuck. Please don't listen to it. That voice is the devil who comes and stomps on your head, telling you that you're not good enough. It is so easy to let our negative Nancys come out to play when this is how we feel on the inside, but you have to remind yourself that your negative thoughts do not define you. They will pass and your comeback will always be stronger than the setback. So many people suffer because they listen to each and every single word and believe it is who they are, worshipping the devil.

When it gets a bit too much, hold yourself more tightly, speak gently and do something kind for yourself, just as you would for a friend. Run yourself a bath, light your candles, make another one of your delicious coffees. Whatever makes you smile, do more of that when you feel down. Play your favourite music and watch yourself automatically singing along. Take a walk, get some fresh air, play a podcast or read a book. Do more of the things that make you forget about the chaos. If you find it hard to find anything that brings you joy, take up a new hobby. Ask yourself what has inspired you lately.

Fill up your free time with little balls of happiness that make you smile. Don't push yourself further away when you feel sad – use that energy to give yourself more love. Treat yourself with so much kindness it scares your demons off. Do one kind thing for yourself when your mood drops, whatever that may be. It will pull you through to tomorrow. Then when tomorrow arrives it will bring forward a new you.

Write yourself love notes

Every night before I go to bed I get my journal out and write myself love notes for the following day. When I open up the page the next morning and see these messages it starts my day on a whole new level. It is so beautiful to see. I challenge you to sit and reflect every evening and prepare messages for yourself for the next day. If you have had a challenging day, write yourself a message for the next morning. 'Today is a new day and I am going to let go of what happened yesterday. Today is going to be a great day!' or 'I am so proud of you – keep going.' These little reminders will programme your mindset and they are the perfect tool for boosting your self-esteem. Be your own cheerleader, cheer yourself on. Nobody will do it better than you. A beautiful day begins with a boost of confidence, a grateful heart and a beautiful mindset.

I love who I am

For all my mistakes, I forgive you.

I care for who I am,

The woman I am growing to be.

My heart deserves nothing but…

Love for all that I am,

Who I am.

You are more than enough

It was how she picked herself back up when she didn't feel good enough. It was her voice that saved her, that brought her back to the realisation that she was enough – more than enough. She chose not to listen to the tricks her mind played on her, and that's where she outgrew her old self. In that moment of believing, that faith bounced her back. On the days she didn't feel good, she reminded herself of who she was, and that's what life's all about – reminding ourselves of who we are and what we are capable of achieving. Because you, my darling, are more than enough.

'I hope you know how magical you are.'

@rewiringthoughts_

One day you have life and the next you don't

'You can check your bank account to see how much money you have, but you can't check to see how much time you have left.'

@rewiringthoughts_

Is the title of the final chapter painful to read, or powerful to read, or both? Whatever you thought, it's the truth. Death comes knocking on everyone's door. I know some of you are thinking, 'Oh no, why is she talking about this?' Who would ever want to go deeply into this topic? That is the barrier we need to break. We need to have the ability to come to terms with what happens to us all. Most of the world sees death as the worst possible thing, but it can be turned into a positive instead of fearing it. That was once my perception of death: fear. I would have sleepless nights, worrying myself to sleep over the thought that one day I won't be here. Not able to see my loved ones, not able to give them a hug, not able to laugh or dance ever again. Thoughts of my own funeral and people attending gave my whole body chills, as it dawned on me that my life would one day become a distant memory.

I would have sleepless nights lying on my back, staring at the ceiling, unable to shake off the fear of death. I constantly tossed and turned, feeling nauseous with worry. It left me deflated and with the world on my shoulders. The worst thing was that it was a complete waste of time. I knew I had to face my demons or they would become overpowering. I needed to confront myself and ask: 'What is it that makes you so scared of dying?' The answer was that I didn't want to look back on life and know I could have done more and been more. This reply hit me hard; the water works came flooding. I was emotional. The tears started to stream down my face as my whole body was shaking. I couldn't stop, until all of a sudden I felt a sense of calm come over me. It was my inner voice, comforting me with a soft 'Worry less. Have more faith and it will all happen for you.' I stopped crying and began to smile, overcoming my fear there and then. Fear is just an emotion and, just like the others, it will pass. From then, I had an open mind to speak on the subject of death and, if anything, it motivates me to live each day as if it is my last. It is a hard lesson to grasp, but we must take every opportunity that comes our way and grab it with both hands. Laugh louder, love harder and leave your mark on this world.

Don't let the thought of death scare you, my friend. You were chosen to be put on this earth, so reap its rewards. There will never be another masterpiece created quite like you. Your originality shines so brightly that, I promise you, all the answers you have been searching for will definitely come. Time is still ticking and it isn't going to stop for anybody, because we are all heading to the same destination, so stop dwelling too much. Don't let life make you take it so seriously. See it as a bundle of fun with challenges. Let this message I share with you ignite a fire in your belly to get you started; forgive people, and move on with love. Don't hold any hate in your heart. Just let whatever happened yesterday go. Wash the dirt from your hands and stand tall, with your chin pointing to the sky, with nothing to hide, and be proud of who you really are, because the world needs more of that. Too many people change because they feel embarrassed to show their rawness, but I am certain this version of you is the missing part of the puzzle.

Being alive is a gift; to wake up every morning is the single greatest reward you will ever receive from this earth. That alone makes me want to say: congratulations, you are alive today! What you are going through is preparing you for what's next. Regret will hurt more than not trying, so don't wait for this feeling of belief to come and go – just start. You are here to enjoy life, to face those fears head on and create life exactly how you want it. Go and try today, because that alone will give you something to look back and smile about. Life is no dress rehearsal, so don't treat it like one. Make this show the best one of all time, because it's all you've got. One day you have life and the next you don't.

The world is yours

Quit that job, start that business, book that holiday, read that book, get up out of bed today and wash your hair! Dance around your house naked (if you wish), drink endless amounts of coffee, watch your favourite movie over and over again. Learn a new language, dump that toxic ex, catch those flights, look above the clouds, chase those sunsets, run along the beach, get your feet stuck in the sand, feel that breeze, smell those flowers, learn how to cook, bake those cakes, make a campfire in your garden, hike more, venture more, date again, get married again, laugh again, kiss again, bring your silly side out and shake off your serious side. Change your life when you aren't happy and remember that this world is yours. You are free and able to do anything your heart desires. There is so much to live for. Go and chase after your world – it's waiting for you to wake up. It's time to spread your wings – you are ready to fly now, beautiful.

Your time

It's time to feel the sun shine on your face again.

It's time to get yourself out of the darkness.

It's time to work harder than you ever have before.

It's time to make this life the one you won't regret as it's the only one, for sure, you will remember.

My love, it's time.

'Being alive is a gift in itself. Count your blessings everyday.'

@rewiringthoughts_

It has always been within you

~~~~~~~~~~~~~~~~~~~~~~~~~~~~~~~~~~

Every answer you need,

Every friend you search for,

All the strength you can't find,

All the love you crave is already within.

You are all you need.

It has always been you.

The ending

During the time spent writing this book I have shed a lot of tears – happy ones, of course! I am so blessed that I have found my purpose in life so I could get to you all more quickly. I pray my journey and words have helped you in some way. Come back to the pages that made you feel alive and please share them with a friend or loved one. Be their light, and let's save one soul at a time. I would love to see you tag @rewiringthoughts_ sharing your favourite page of this book. I will be so excited to hear from you all. I want to say thank you to my wonderful family and dearest friends. Thank you for being my angels. I dedicate this book to you all and to all of you beautiful lot, my readers. I owe this to each and every single one of you. If my words can save just one person, then I have done my job.

I hope you have found this book a reason for you to heal and to start looking within. I hope this book has given you that boost of confidence to just go for it, no matter how stuck you feel. Even if you don't follow what I have set out in this book religiously, don't worry. As long as you have balance, life will be just as good as you want it to be. I hope the penny has dropped, so that you realise how special you are. Most of all, I hope my words and story have shone a light on your soul. The journey started when you opened this book, and now that you are closing it, I am excited for you to unleash your true potential with the power you hold. Never forget how important you are, and remember, you can become the person you dare to be and do the things you have always dreamed of doing.

The world is yours, my dear.

Lots of love,
Kate x